BATHROOMS

Diane Dorrans Saeks

CHRONICLE BOOKS
SAN FRANCISCO

For my gorgeous son, Justin, with love, always. — D.D.S.

Printed in Hong Kong

Book and Cover Design:
Madeleine Corson Design, San Francisco

Cover Photograph:
A bathroom in Los Angeles by Michael Berman.
Photography by Jeremy Samuelson.

Title Page:
A sparkling bathroom in Los Angeles.
Photography by Jeremy Samuelson.

Library of Congress Cataloging-in-Publication Data available.

ISBN 0-8118-1334-7

Distributed in Canada by:
Raincoast Books
8680 Cambie Street
Vancouver BC V6P 6M9

10 9 8 7 6 5 4 3 2 1

Chronicle Books
85 Second Street
San Francisco
California 94105
Web Site: www.chronbooks.com

WATER MUSIC: THE JOYS OF BATHING

Sensuality, Cleanliness. Beauty. Well-being. In a world where aromatherapy candles, extravagantly scented and soothing soaps, luscious towels, sybaritic bathrobes, and elaborate showerheads are among the best-sellers, bathrooms really matter. They have become a haven from the hubbub, a resplendent refuge, and a chamber for dreaming and reviving. Certainly, bathrooms are no longer the puritanical places in which pleasure was prohibited and jollity unthinkable. With variable-jet whirlpool baths now common, 32-jet adjustable showers available, soaking tubs de rigueur, hand-held personal showers increasingly in demand, and shower/steam cabinets on the march into America's bathrooms, the bath today pampers the body and encourages health and happiness. ⚲ Bathroom suites are often planned for sheer practicality and hospital-like efficiency and hygiene, but today's best are always elegantly simple. ⚲ Planning bathroom decor requires introspection and soul-searching. While some people are happiest in laboratory-like white rooms with gleaming tiles and spotless tile floors, others long for romantic escapes festooned with balloon shades and elaborate shower curtains and perhaps an Oriental rug. One person's idea of luxury may depend on total understatement. For him or her, the creamy limestone floor, white fixtures, big white bath, and unembellished white walls afford peace and quiet and room for reflection. For others, an old-fashioned claw-foot tub, an elaborate antique dresser or armoire, and embroidered white draperies, along with a vintage washbasin (or a pair) mean instant heaven. Even a tiny bathroom or a petite powder room can have style. Included on these pages are small-room tips, ideas for remodeling, and inspiration from some of California's top designers and architects. ⚲ Honed marble, French limestone, soapstone, cherrywood, and tempered glass are luxurious choices. Retro styles of fittings and fixtures reminiscent of grand old London hotels and Parisian luxury suites are being installed in more and more American bathrooms. While pared-down, classic new fixtures by designers like Philippe Starck display clean lines that work in both contemporary and traditional-style rooms, many designers forgo sleek efficiency for pie-plate-like chrome showerheads, elaborate Edwardian nickel-plated valves, and serpentine curves of brass faucets looped with snake-like hand-held showers. Rather than turning a bathroom into a "machine for living," homeowners are bringing in antique armoires and installing vintage Orient-Express-style towel racks. A terry-cloth-covered chaise longue, exercise equipment, a meditation mat all lift the spirit. Time lavished on oneself in the bathroom is time well spent. OPPOSITE Clean lines: A simple, luxurious bathroom in Southern California.

STYLE PORTFOLIO

All we really need for a wonderful bath and complete relaxation are steamy, hot water, a candle or two, a slippery bar of soap — and time to enjoy them. But then if the bathroom has style and panache — and is wonderfully functional — the experience is a magical one we want to repeat over and over. Good bathroom design should be appropriate — to the spirit of the architecture, to the place, to its purpose — and it should uplift and delight those who use it. For some, that means the heft and grandeur of an old Edwardian pedestal. For others, it's an ultra-modern glass basin, a sensual, sculptural faucet, or a soaking tub. Today's priceless luxuries are beautiful light (night and day), sexy surfaces, and easily maintained materials (brushed metals, glossy tiles, old-fashioned porcelain). Just be sure to make the bathroom a place where you'll sing, dream, read, write, and plan great things.

OPPOSITE   Pristine white: A wall of glass blocks capture light into this inviting bathroom.

Actor Jami Gertz (a shining presence on top television show *ER* and in the movie *Twister*) has complete faith in her interior designer, Kerry Joyce. Gertz and her husband, investment banker Antony Ressler, have been working with him for years and trust his judgment in matters of style, proportion, color, materials, and furnishing. (Joyce has his own collection of furniture, manufactured by James Jennings' company in Los Angeles.) ⚲ When they set out to build their new family house in Beverly Hills, Gertz and Ressler knew it would look like an elegant twenties country house, and that it would have wood floors, but beyond that they left the details up to Joyce. The designer is noted for the pale palette of his rooms, the sculptural purity of his furniture, and the somewhat held-back, understated effect of his decor. ⚲ For Gertz's bathroom, Joyce's scenario was that the new white-on-white room should look as if it had been kept in a pristine state since the twenties. "I wanted to evoke the twenties without looking hackneyed," said Joyce. He selected classic fixtures and fittings: a two-person porcelain cast-iron tub, nickel-plated faucets and handles, and shiny white marble with subtle markings. "Bathrooms are one place where shiny marble is appropriate. It's right for a period look, and it's easy to maintain." ⚲ Perhaps this bathroom is most instructive concerning what Joyce did not select. The designer knows that luxury often whispers — and that glamor may be found in superb craftsmanship, reassuringly comfortable furniture, and a marble floor that's beautiful enough to tap-dance on. His direction: nothing flashy, no overly modern gestures. Each material, light fixture, drapery rod, and fixture here is somewhat understated and certainly very low-key for a bathroom in the luscious landscape of Beverly Hills. The custom-made drapery rod is a simple sketch of metal — a mere silhouette of a thing, but efficient nonetheless. The ebony-black chair of Joyce's design is a rather straightforward affair but it's dressed with a ruffled terry cloth seat with sculptural lines. There's no visual clutter, nothing to jangle the nerves. ⚲ The clean-lined simplicity and pure comfort of the house so pleased Gertz and Ressler that Joyce is now working on a new house for the couple. This time the house is again rather monochromatic and superbly detailed — but in the style of a Louisiana plantation house.

OPPOSITE Tap dance: The generous sculpted form of Kohler's handsome
"Vintage" bath is a voluptuous presence in the all-white bathroom. Joyce dressed the
windows in gauzy white-dotted Swiss cotton draperies. The floor is rare
white statuary marble with a very fine grain.

California interior designers, like their counterparts in other states, often find themselves renovating and remodeling bathrooms that are a mere ten years old. So they learn a thing or two about which colors and materials date, which fixtures work best, which materials hold up, and above all, how to create new bathrooms with some longevity. ⚭ For clients who were adding a wing to their house, Michael Berman designed the interior decor for a new bedroom and an L-shaped bathroom. ⚭ "My client had two requests," remembered Berman. "The first was that she wanted a fireplace in the bathroom, like ones she had seen in Europe. The second was that she wanted to be able to see her beloved garden from the bathtub." Berman and architect Jesse Castaneda fulfilled both requests and gave their clients a romantic and practical bathroom. ⚭ The house was designed in the manner of a Tuscan villa, but Berman wanted the bathroom to be more pared-down and reminiscent of a grand old classic Italian hotel. "It has the luxury of all-modern fixtures and comfort, but with historical references," said the designer. The color palette is soft-ivory, white, camel, wheat, and limestone. Berman avoided fashion colors and "trend-of-the-month" tones — knowing they date fast. Still, all surfaces are very functional. Polished marble and honed limestone add to the timeless look. ⚭ Every square inch of this bathroom was carefully considered and planned. One particularly practical idea was to inset glass wall shelves at each end of the bath. Here the homeowner can stack towels, *objets d'art,* and books and magazines. (Some homeowners who love to watch old movies or favorite television shows in the bath would probably place a television set — very securely — on the lower shelf. Such luxury!) Not only do the shelves offer useful storage space, they make the room

appear wider. Since the homeowner wanted views of the green landscape just outside, Berman and Castenada selected a window of clear glass — not frosted. It's a sensible choice, and one to be emulated when privacy is assured. Berman also noted that today it is essential to design a luxury bathroom that is entirely practical and very quick to clean.

OPPOSITE & ABOVE Taking the plunge: From the oval-shaped whirlpool tub, the owners of this Los Angeles bathroom can view the citrus trees and clipped parterres in their Italian-style garden. The floor is French Baumanier limestone set in a parquet pattern. Counters and the tub surround are white "Biancono" marble. Michael Berman designed cabinets with drawers and pull-out makeup trays. Architecture: Jesse Castaneda, Malibu.

Turning a chopped-up series of small rooms into a gracious his-and-hers bathroom was not exactly a snap for designer Suzanne Tucker — but she applied her many years of experience to every detail. The result is an unusually handsome suite, complete with doors to a sunny outdoor terrace and fine views of the Marin Headlands and the outer reaches of San Francisco Bay. ⚲ "Given such a long, narrow, tight space, I tried to create a semblance of privacy for both the occupants," said Tucker. "We wanted the bathroom to be as gracious and practical as possible." ⚲ The second floor of the 1924 Mediterranean-style house had been remodeled over the years, and little detail remained in the bathroom suite. Tucker had custom cabinetry made, and a pair of bow-fronted vanities with narrow drawers on each side opposite the bath. "I didn't have the luxury of making deep cabinets, so the bow fronts have presence without pressing into the room," noted Tucker. "These rooms are just nine feet wide, so it's important to command and expand the space." Instead of small tiles, Tucker used larger slabs of travertine to give the room a sense of graciousness and a grander feeling. ⚲ This bathroom is full of subtle (but telling) details and perfectly illustrates how a remodel should be tackled. First, when beginning a renovation or restyle it is essential to look closely at the architecture of the house, its style, its mood, its ambiance, its setting. Straying too far from the heartbeat of the house — jamming a modern bathroom into a woodsy Arts & Crafts house, for example — is always a mistake. Foisting a frou-frou Victorian bathroom into a Modernist house would be foolhardy. The bathroom can be updated, but it should have echoes of its actual history. Existing light should be examined and pondered. Should windows be larger? Can the bathroom be extended? Can fixtures be removed or replaced? This bathroom was gutted and reconfigured to make it comfortable and private for two people. Never rush into a remodel. ⚲ Among the delights for the eye here are a rare eighteenth-century Italian lacquered mirror with an elaborate parcel gilt crest, a pair of Venetian twisted crystal candlestick lamps with silver beaded shades, and an English bell jar lantern light fixture. A subdued taupe and pale gold Khotan carpet, late eighteenth-century, covers the honed travertine floor. ⚲ Antiques — Venetian candlestick lamps, a Swedish neoclassical parcel-gilt armchair upholstered in Fortuny fabric — give the room a certain elegance.

OPPOSITE Master plan: This elegant Sea Cliff bathroom was carved from a series of poky little rooms by designer Suzanne Tucker. The vanities and floor are honed Italian cross-cut ivory travertine. In the pullman-shaped room, she included a man's dressing room, a woman's dressing room, a bathing area, two vanities, and lots of storage.

In the northern reaches of the Napa Valley, hidden behind high oleander hedges and a grove of olive trees, stands a remarkable private house that few explorers will ever see. The striking sandstone residence was recently given an imaginative renovation by San Francisco architectural firm Kuth Ranieri, working with architect Jim Jennings. ☿ Byron Kuth and Elizabeth Ranieri decided that the best course of action would be to improve and update the whole circa-1880, 6,000-square-foot structure. They completely gutted the interior. The owner wanted all of the seismic-upgrade bracing and support systems to be invisible and to preserve the old local stone walls. ☿ To draw light into the interior, the architects replaced the old roof and built new skylights around the perimeter. Now sunlight casts three-dimensional patterns on the stone walls and slants across the floor. In the process, they achieved two fine ideals of the great architect Louis Kahn: silence and light. ☿ "Everything we were going to put in had to have authenticity and integrity," said Ranieri. "It's one thing to design a beautiful interior, but it gains its value by its practicality and by its grace and enhancement of everyday life." ☿ The craggy sandstone, so tactile and archetypal, combined well with the contemporary vocabulary of the renovation. Smooth, rather modernist shapes and sensual contours of fixtures are perfectly at home with the rough-hewn rocks and the rural site. ☿ "The pure joy of working on this residence was obsessing about every single detail — the grand concepts as well as door pulls, window latches, floor finishes, and faucets," said Elizabeth Ranieri. "In the best architecture, absolutely everything must work to its optimum, as well as give great pleasure." ☿ Honoring the rock walls, the architects placed fixtures carefully so as not to obscure their rugged

beauty. The bathroom is fitted with easy-to-clean counters, easy-access sinks, an almost monastic bathing area, and a luxurious chaise longue. Lighting for the residence was designed by Melinda Morrison. Here are two architects in full command of their materials. Stone — timeless and reassuring — is the perfect foil for thick cast-glass counters.

OPPOSITE & ABOVE Bathing beauty: Sandstone walls, original to the circa 1880 house, are evocative of Napa Valley's rich history. Architects Byron Kuth and his wife, Elizabeth Ranieri, planned a renovated bathroom that is both practical and poetic.

When San Francisco interior designer Alice Wiley began remodeling her own house, she conducted the same kind of in-depth research she would normally do for her clients. "I did a lot of looking and inquiring, because, as I tell my clients, you're only doing this bathroom once and it has to be right," she said. "It also should be the best quality you can afford." She was working with a budget, just like her clients, she said. ☿ She and her husband, executive Peter Hall, had acquired their 1885 house in 1996. The Queen Anne Victorian had formerly been the guesthouse for a neighboring mansion. The couple and their son-in-law, architect Rob Wilkinson, redesigned the three-bedroom, three-bathroom house to carve out a new office, a new guest room/library, and a new private bathroom and dressing room adjoining their new bedroom. ☿ "We wanted a gracious master bedroom suite, designed so that we could talk as we began our days and relax at the end of the evening," said Wiley. "A structure wall divides the bathroom from the walk-in dressing room, so we made the bathroom large — 14 feet by 14 feet — because otherwise it would have been a series of smallish rooms." ☿ The space for the new bathroom and dressing room was built out on a former open deck. The full project — adding the new bathroom (and a kitchen beneath it), restyling the bedroom (with a new fireplace), plus other changes in the structure — took about eight months, from planning and permits to completion. ☿ "We wanted the bathroom to be very sunny, with views of the garden," said Wiley. "I also wanted it to have architectural detail." ☿ "My wish list included two sinks, high ceilings, and a large oval tub," Wiley recalled. "My dream bathroom included plenty of counter space, drawers so that hair dryers and cosmetics could be put away, and storage for

makeup and toiletries." ☿ For six months Wiley studied every aspect of bathrooms. "I looked at every residential bathroom I could, read magazines, read design books, visited showrooms, and looked at every available style," she said. She also talked to friends who had renovated their bathrooms and asked questions.

OPPOSITE & ABOVE San Francisco interior designer Alice Wiley chose Concinnity's Citation Beaded hardware in polished nickel from D.J. Mehler. The floor is Baumanier limestone laid in a Versailles-inspired grid. The tub is by American Standard. Gauze curtains can be closed for privacy. The walls were glazed pale apricot by San Francisco decorative painter Willem Racke. The architecture is by Rob Wilkinson, Wilkinson & Hartman, San Rafael.

When interior designer Mary Wood and her husband, Steve, built their new house in Los Olivos, they gave it the landscape-embracing broad verandahs of colonial-era Australian farmhouses. They also set their 26-foot by 18-foot bedroom up on the second floor, and furnished it like a living room, with a beautiful fireplace, a desk and computer, and a claw-foot tub, painted cinnabar. From the bath, they can view merlot and chardonnay vineyards, among the oldest in the Santa Ynez Valley. ⚲ "We put the bath in one corner of the bedroom rather than in the bathroom because we wanted to be able to see the fireplace and the view," said Mary, known to her friends as Dede. Steve recently retired from his post as a lieutenant ocean lifeguard for Los Angeles County. Their house stands among 500-year-old oaks, and their boundaries are delineated by pleached rows of whispering cottonwoods. ⚲ The house was designed with great simplicity so that most of the budget was spent on quality materials and craftsmanship. In the bathroom adjacent to the bedroom, Wood used simple, classic materials — plain white tiles, white ceramic pedestal sinks (raised on two-inch cherry wood bases), and thick cherry wood countertops. The Woodses put in the one-inch-thick cherry wood floors themselves and applied a nontoxic, ecologically correct water-based sealant. ⚲ Mary Wood knows the value of beginning with perfectly proportioned architecture — nothing awkward or ungainly or tricky. The lovely balance of her windows and the rhythm they create as they march around the room will be as pleasing fifty or a hundred years on. "This is a contemporary house but it doesn't scream 'new,'" said the designer. And staying true to the modest spirit of the Australian farmhouses that inspired this residence, the couple kept moldings, trim, and paint treatments in balance, never allowing finishes to become too decorative or eccentric. This is a house that truly belongs to its country site. ⚲ "We wake up in the morning to views of miles of vineyards," said Mary. There's no sound, save for the wind in the oaks and the eucalyptus leaves. "Looking out from every window of the house is the best part," said Steve. "We sit in the bathroom, talking things over, looking out at the line of cottonwoods changing color in the sunset." ⚲ "We're quite remote, so it's very dark here at night, and the stars look so close," said Mary. "We watch the moon rise from our windows and listen to the stillness. The beauty of nature surrounds us."

OPPOSITE Country comforts: Two hundred yards of white cotton pique (on pewter curtain rods) make up the double-layer full draperies in Mary and Steve Wood's upstairs bedroom suite. Corner windows are stock 36-inch by 72-inch by Kolbe Kolbe.

Patrick Wade and David DeMattei believe that the loftiest purpose of travel is to discover antiques, art, and vintage treasures of other cultures. The two executives, who spend most of the year in New York, have chosen to create the perfect setting to house these treasures. Polished bathroom countertops of cream/sienna marble, pristine shelves, antique-style light fixtures, and handsome chairs make perfect landing places for books, alabaster urns, Merchant-Ivory-esque etchings, framed historic photographs, carvings, and French paintings. And the renovated bathroom suite is no exception. ☿ When Wade and DeMattei moved into the beautifully proportioned Edwardian house, layers of paint and the ad hoc renovations of 80 years had been cleared. They cleaned up the design, modernized it with a light touch, but kept all the original moldings and doors. "Putting together a room so that it is cohesive and pleasing is all about careful editing and placement," said their friend Stephen Brady, who helped with the redesign. "Rooms should never look jumbled or fussy. Each piece of furniture, each accessory, should be beautifully presented so that you can really appreciate it." ☿ Instead of heavy-handed Edwardian bathroom fittings, Wade chose nickel-

plated light fixtures with a turn-of-the-century feeling — with white glass shades. Frosted shell sconces add muted light. Mirrors are framed with white lacquered moldings. ☿ "We never wanted the decor to look 'decorated' or predictable or period," said Wade. "Odd proportions are much more intriguing than safe and expected combinations." God, of course, is in the details. Mirrors are beveled, marble counters are bowed, pulls feel smooth to the hand, cabinet doors are beautifully shaped. There's a hint of Edwardiana in the pair of retro-style wall sconces that is echoed in the nickel-plated shaving mirror and the quirky display shelves. But everything does not have to be Olde Worlde. Faucets are efficient, modern designs, and wash bowls are simple easy-to-clean rounds. ☿ "I sometimes imagine the very proper Edwardian family who built this house returning for a visit," mused Wade. "I think they would feel at home."

OPPOSITE & ABOVE Visual stimulation: Collections of antique reading glasses, French silver vases, English ironstone, and colognes and candles are displayed against a pale, creamy background. Installing faucets on the side of the bowl saves crucial inches in this narrow space. Curved counters give the room a more gracious feeling.

Designing a room without the influence of fashions or fads is a noble effort — and only time will tell if it was truly successful. In early 1970, Dr. Leo Keoshian, a noted hand surgeon, commissioned San Francisco interior designer John Dickinson to design new interiors for his twenties Spanish-style house. Built on a quiet tree-lined street in Palo Alto by architecture professor Clarence Tantau, the house has a well-mannered, perfectly symmetrical floor plan and daylong light. ☿ "John's plan from the beginning was to keep the rooms very precise, quite understated," recalled Dr. Keoshian. Several tones of white were Dickinson's choice for the rooms' colors. He preferred white in all its shades because it does not draw attention to itself and it never goes out of style. ☿ Even in designing the bathroom, John Dickinson did not put originality on a pedestal. Logic and function come first, he said. A steel tub, which stands in the center of the light-filled room, is an example of Dickinson's use of somewhat utilitarian materials. He made sheet steel, plaster, industrial wool carpet, and simple white-lacquered surfaces seem utterly luxurious and sensual. To perfect the curves of the three-foot by seven-foot bath, Dickinson first had the metal craftsman create a

sample corner. Finally, welded immaculately and given a silken polish, the seamless steel feels sensuous and luxurious. ☿ The plumbing for the iconic bath had to be carefully thought through. Hot water is routed through pipes under the bath and through the towel rack to warm the metal bath — and the towels. There is no water spout, simply a round outlet for the water to exit with considerable pressure. ☿ "It was important that the water should pour out with some authority," noted Dickinson. Tap handles in brass were made to look like gold nuggets. ☿ Beyond the wall of white-lacquered closets and the dressing area is a shower. The two-tone flat wool carpet is outlined with a tailored border of garnet and off-white. Arranged beside the bath — and in an intriguing juxtaposition with its rigorous geometries — is a hand-painted plaster table, designed by John Dickinson. Also of note: views of an enclosed garden can be glimpsed through curtained French doors.

OPPOSITE & ABOVE Liquid asset: This renovated and redesigned Northern California bathroom, with its alluring steel bath and balanced proportions, is one of John Dickinson's most innovative designs. Part of its appeal is the juxtaposition of materials: wool carpet with steel, bronze with plaster, smooth white lacquer cabinets with "distressed plaster" walls hand-painted by Carol Lansdown.

The Southern California bathroom of antiques dealer/interior designer Andrew Virtue may be no bigger than an afterthought, but it is as carefully composed as a Shakespearean sonnet. There are lessons to be learned from this Southern California designer's approach and his handling of even the small details. This is not one-note, theme design — Virtue was never following preset guidelines — but rather the very knowing approach of a keen connoisseur of antiques, art, and French and English decor. Experimentation will always keep design lively, unexpected, and fresh, noted Virtue. On a pair of nineteenth-century gilt wood brackets, Virtue has placed a pair of nineteenth-century blue and white Chinese vases, juxtaposed with forties turquoise art pottery. Within this parameter, he has deployed a framed contemporary sketch, a forties seascape, Neapolitan water scenes, an Italian gouache of Capri, a photograph of a Mazatlan resort in a gilt frame, and a thirties English seascape. Some of them, he said, are really too good to be in a steamy bathroom, but he likes to look at them every day. ☿ "I like things that exude atmosphere, even if they are not technically correct," noted Virtue. "Funny and esoteric combinations are always more interesting. I never mind cracks. I almost love things more if they've been smashed and stuck back together again." ☿ Measuring just six feet by eight feet, the bathroom looks beyond fragrant trumpet vines and an old eucalyptus to a lavish garden. "It's wonderful to have a sense of boundless nature just outside," said the designer, who owns Virtue, an antiques and design shop in Los Angeles. "It's essential for a small room to have views of the great outdoors — otherwise, it would be quite claustrophobic." ☿ Light spills into the room all day through standard twenties wood sash windows. Virtue, never deterred by banal architecture, has dressed his windows with plain white muslin and sheer draperies, sewn by his mother, V'etta Virtue. "She's a brilliant seamstress," exclaimed Virtue. "You should have seen the Halloween costumes she made for me when I was growing up." ☿ Without forcing the theme, Virtue's bathroom suggests an English seaside hotel in Edwardian times. He capitalized on the twenties sink with porcelain levers and faucet — and the medicine cabinet, also original to the building. "They're a bit temperamental, but it's worth putting up with them to have the feeling of being in an old building," Virtue said.

OPPOSITE Water features: Andrew Virtue positioned entertainment for the eyes on the walls of his tiny bathroom. The faux-bamboo Regency-style chair is a perfect place for towels. Simple draperies in white cotton frame the window.

Los Angeles interior and furniture designer Michael Berman is a forties aficionado, as his longtime client food guru Merrill Shindler knows all too well. (Berman is also a thirties aficionado.) When Shindler acquired his Rafael Soriano Case Study house, designed in 1949, he commissioned Berman to renovate and update it in the spirit of Soriano. ⚲ "It's a minimalist house, spare and unpretentious, but it had been given a very boring, predictable remodel in the sixties and looked sadly dated," said Berman. "It was a sea of nondescript beige floor tiles and beige laminate cabinetry." ⚲ Berman found the blueprints of Soriano's design in the Soriano archives and took cues from the original drawings. "It's very compact, so I selected teak for the cabinetry, sheet linoleum for the floor, and kept the room simple and ethereal," Berman said. The owners collect black-and-white photography, so the room makes a quiet background to the framed works. ⚲ Berman, also seized by the spirit of Japanese baths, chose slabs of dove-gray limestone for the countertop and for the wall behind the bath. The French stone, with its pale markings and suggestion of ancient landscapes, is a handsome counterpoint to the teak cabinets and steel-framed windows. ⚲ Faucets and valves are brushed nickel. The combination of their subtle sheen with the matte finish of the honed stone gives the room a rich, tactile quality. ⚲ Berman got his clients started on a collection of Roseville, Bauer, and Catalina art pottery, and favorite pieces are displayed on a series of teak shelves suspended on one wall. The shelves are also used for white towels. ⚲ Berman, of course, was confronting head-on the kind of redesign that faces many homeowners. Great numbers of family houses were built throughout California in the forties and fifties, and they're still favored today for their open and airy style, simple room

plans, and comfort. But kitchens and bathrooms invariably present problems. If these houses have been renovated (typically in the sixties or seventies), they have a dated air. If they have not been touched by an architect or designer since they were built, amenities are often skimpy. Michael Berman's wise approach — luxurious materials used with restraint.

OPPOSITE & ABOVE Case study: Michael Berman reworked and updated the Rafael Soriano-designed bathroom with the spare lines and unpretentious spirit of the forties original. He gave it a sense of comfort and luxury that the machine-made-ethic room never had. Outlets and appliances are hidden in the medicine cabinet.

Design Workbook

Bathroom design, renovation, and restyling all offer an adventure and a challenge. Here, some of the top architects and designers in California lead the novice remodeler through all the steps of renovation. Their opinions, based on years of experience, can save time and money. And they do not speak with one voice. One expert prefers a high-quality resin bath; another insists that only cast-iron will do. A noted architect specifies honed marble for the floor for safety; a designer likes the squeaky-clean look of shiny marble. And while some designers insist that all fittings or fixtures must match, others warm to a more eclectic look of vintage fittings in a handsome new shower cabinet, or elaborate old salvaged sconces juxtaposed with a super-sleek contemporary bath. Learn from these experts, gain from their knowledge, and educate your eye. OPPOSITE   Design: Robert Frear.

WORKING WITH A BATHROOM DESIGNER/ARCHITECT

Working as a team on the project will produce the best results. Clear communication with the contractor is important, too.

Designer David Rivera and architectural designer Eugene Nahemow, with Lamperti Associates in San Rafael, have designed hundreds of bathrooms. They believe that candid and open discussions are important at the beginning of the project.

Clients should be straightforward about their needs, and about their budget. "It is important to decide on fundamentals that cannot be compromised," said Rivera. "Sometimes, for a client, the big picture can get lost in all the tiny details. A designer or contractor should always have objectivity, an overview." Here, Nahemow and Rivera help renovators through the process.

Getting Started

How do you find a designer, an architect, or (later) a contractor? Ask your friends. Visit decorator showcase houses. Check magazines. Decide which kind of professional you can afford — and the extent of the work required. There are architects, contractors with in-house designers, construction companies with in-house architects, builders, certified bathroom designers, cabinetry companies that design bathrooms, and decorators.

Beginning

Discuss materials and products in depth with the professional. Talk about your tastes, likes and dislikes, and needs. Be honest about your budget. Get a good dialogue going. Discuss what's new on the market, how much it costs. Don't go directly to the contractor. He will be happy to see you, but there will be no resolution until drawings are refined.

Research

Look through showrooms with the designer/architect. Glean information about new fixtures, fittings, styles, and materials. Get a sense of design directions, new looks, new ideas.

Site

The designer/architect will visit the bathroom to be remodeled. He or she should completely evaluate the room, check the construction, examine fixtures, check lighting.

Budgets

Costs should be examined in detail. This is a time for realistic examination of goals. This is also the time to balance expectations and budget. Look at ways the cost may be trimmed — or ideas reworked. Start to discuss options. Look for inventive solutions to problems. Talk about budget breakdowns.

Design

At this stage, a fee will be paid for design. Then you will move to bids, and to selecting a contractor. Architects and designers will often recommend a contractor. Examine all bids — but be sure to nail down the exact specifications, complete

---

OPPOSITE The doctor is in: Radio doctor Dean Edell's renovated bathroom in San Rafael. Design: Lamperti Associates.

with tile, baths, and other materials. The architects will also be supplying paperwork for permit applications.

Contractors

Go and look at the work of several local contractors if possible. Look for best-quality jobs — and for contractors who will be collaborative. You need good management, reliable staff, good crews, and a contractor who is accessible and reliable. Choose people you like — they will be in your house for weeks.

Progress

After the contract is signed and the deposit paid, the contractor will give you a work schedule. All permits will need to be finalized. Spell out exactly what the architect's responsibility will be. Is there a fee for work "observation"? If the plans must be adjusted, how will problems be resolved?

Completion

When the work is completed (see The Steps of a Remodel, page 37), inspect every aspect of the bathroom with the designer or architect. Write up a list of anything that needs to be delivered or fixed, and be sure that all materials are as specified.

OPPOSITE White and creamy hues – versatile and timeless – are generally the wisest color choices for bathrooms. Here, skylights pour light into the shower and bath.

BELOW Details of Dr. Dean Edell's bathroom. Simple cabinetry, marble counters, and tile floors afford efficient maintenance. Design: Lamperti Associates.

THE COST OF A REMODEL

What can you get for your money? Here is a rough estimate. Note that California urban centers tend to be more expensive and that the cost of labor and materials may be less in other parts of the country.

$3,000 AND UNDER On this budget, the layout will stay intact. Most updates will be cosmetic, but considerable improvements can be made. It's possible to visit a home center and get advice on installing a new floor, repainting walls, replacing cabinets, replacing an old laminate counter, installing a new shower door, perhaps a new showerhead. Buy generic white fixtures, a stock tub.

Larger mirrors will make the room feel more spacious.

$5,000 TO $10,000 It is wise to hire a designer or another design professional. Buying a designer's time (around $500 a consultation for specifications and a shopping list) will always pay off. The result will be more polished, more cohesive. The look can be lightened, brightened, and restyled. This may not be a complete overhaul, but distinct improvements can be made. Be imaginative with stock cabinets and basic fixtures. Install a new vanity, higher-quality fittings, a full-length mirror, a new tile floor, new countertops, updated accessories, new

fixtures. Replace old windows. Add a skylight. Use basic tile and add a sense of luxury with marble accents.

$10,000 TO $20,000 At this budget, reconstruction can kick in. An architect and designer should be involved. The floor space can be enlarged. Closets and spare rooms can be taken over. Custom cabinetry can be added, along with new floor surfaces (possibly stone), new counters with a double sink. A separate shower and tub can be installed. Better lighting should be installed, along with radiant in-floor heating, a bidet, a telephone, stereo, and television.

$30,000 PLUS For this budget, you will get a dream bathroom. The contractor can enlarge the bathroom with a bumpout or by taking space from a porch or an adjacent room. An architect or designer can have the room completely demolished and rebuilt. The walls will be insulated, the plumbing upgraded from galvanized to copper pipe, and all new fixtures and fittings installed. New electrical wiring will be added. Marble, limestone, granite, and the highest-quality tiles are options. A whirlpool tub, sauna, exercise area, meditation area, solarium, and steam shower can be installed, but they will eat up a large part of the budget.

THE STEPS OF A REMODEL

You've OK'd the bathroom plans and engaged the contractor. It's all set to go. Now what?

If you've never lived through a remodel, it's impossible to know what will happen. Hint: for several weeks there will loud banging and odd drafts. Big trucks will be parked in the driveway, and the neighbors may get a little tense. Checks will be written. Inspectors will arrive. More banging will ensue. And one day it will all be over. Designer David Rivera of Lamperti Associates in San Rafael describes the ideal progression.

Time

The contract will generally stipulate how much time the contractor expects the project to take. Clauses will also note that the contractor cannot be held responsible for Acts of God or any changes required by codes and building inspectors. Unexpected asbestos removal, for example, could delay the project.

Information

Prior to starting, pick up a package of consumer information to guide you through the thicket of safety issues, health issues, codes, and the local authority's requirements.

Permits

The contractor will apply to the local authorities for building permits. It may take from a week to a month to get them. An experienced remodeler undertaking a minor remodel may be able to get an over-the-counter permit. Typically, fees are charged for permits. The larger the project, the higher the cost — usually a percentage of the total. Design review issues that involve removing a wall or adding a window or that may affect the privacy of neighbors can complicate and delay matters.

Grace Period

After signing the contract, you have a few days to change your mind. The law allows for "buyer's remorse."

Good Neighbors

Alert next-door neighbors before renovation starts. Let them know how long the project will take and warn them of possible noise. It's considerate to disturb nearby houses as little as possible. Being proactive will save anxiety and recrimination later. Contractors often send out a letter advising neighbors of upcoming work.

Planning

Every fixture and fitting should be in the contractor's possession before the floor is ripped up. Delay the start of work until everything is on hand. Even a common product may be out of stock. Waiting for a pedestal en route from New York, cabinets coming from Canada, or a faucet ordered in a special finish can be very frustrating — especially when the bathroom is torn up and work is delayed.

Work Begins

Finally the first day of work arrives. Agree on a staging area for the contractor. He may need to take over half of the garage or use a guest bedroom for building supplies, tools, bathroom fixtures.

O P P O S I T E   Clever planning: Every inch of space was utilized in this bathroom – including a skylit tub.

Move Out

During a major remodel, the bathroom will be out of commission. Consider moving out of the house for a few weeks.

Be Smart

Micromanaging the project can cause problems. Don't try to manage and direct the subcontractors. Talk to the contractor, designer, and architect — keep the chain of command intact.

Delays

Delays will occur. Plumbing supplies may be back-ordered, cabinetry might not be available, tile may be late, marble may be held up. Keep communicating with the contractor.

Inspections

After the rough construction phase and rough plumbing and electrical are done, a building inspection is required before the walls and floor can be closed.

Progress

After the building inspection, sheetrock and sub-floors are put in and finishes are applied. Now the bathroom is starting to take shape, and the beauty of the architecture is revealed. Toilets, faucets, and the shower all start to appear.

Almost There

There is finally a day when lights actually switch on, water pours out of the faucet, the toilet flushes, and the bath can be filled.

Finally

There must be a final sign-off and inspection by building inspectors. This is especially important. The permit must be closed for a title report for resale or refinancing.

Clean-Up

In most contracts, the contractor agrees to leave the bathroom in "broom finish" order — the sawdust swept up, the garage cleaned up, the fixtures dusted off. The best contracting firms will employ a clean-up crew to leave the bathroom spotless. The clean-up won't be free, but it saves removing appliance stickers, cleaning marble, removing dust and grime. If it's a budget job, save a few dollars and do it yourself.

Afterward

When the beautiful new bathroom is finally completed, don't be outraged if the sink has a small leak, a window sticks, or a fan rattles. That happens under the best circumstances. Call the contractor. Keep a good relationship going. Send the final check.

DO-IT-YOURSELF REMODELING

LEARN Take a night-school class or a technical course in aspects of remodeling. Buy how-to books or study at the library.

FIRST STEPS Learn how to turn off the water.

INFORMATION Get some basic tips at a home remodeling center. Learn how to prep walls for painting or prepare subfloors for tile work.

If the preparation is properly executed and the work is done carefully, the finished job will last longer. Even getting guidance on the proper materials and tools to use is very helpful. Get tips, too, on safe and eco-correct paint cleanup. (Don't forget painters' drop cloths to protect fixtures and the floor.)

GO SLOW Read all directions. Follow steps carefully.

Don't rush into tiling, plastering, or painting. (Hint: don't plan this work just before a major family celebration.)

HELP To get the most professional job and finishes, it's probably best to hire a professional – maybe a moonlighting electrician, painter, or tile layer.

WEEKEND It's generally possible to find tradespeople

who will come in on a weekend to help or supervise. Once you've learned a skill, it may come in handy for the next phase of the remodel.

A B O V E Design does not have to be complex to have comfort and charm.

O P P O S I T E Small bathrooms always benefit from luxurious materials. Here, marble makes its mark.

CHOOSING A BATH

Baths today are beautiful. Sculptural and sensuous, they hug the body and encourage relaxation.

Choosing a bath can be tricky. Do you buy a large bath or whirlpool for their resale value? Or is it best to save money and go with a basic, utilitarian model? Is cast-iron the most durable? Or is it time to get with the times and buy resin composite or acrylic baths? Doris Mehler, owner of the DJ Mehler Collections showroom in the San Francisco Design Center, advises clients all day on which bath to purchase. In her professional opinion, acrylic and composition baths are best. They look modern and clean-lined, can be molded to any shape, now have quality finishes, and can be repaired easily. She also believes that since baths are used mostly for relaxation and not for cleansing, the design should be comfortable. Here are her tips on baths.

Perfect Fit

When choosing a bath — plain vanilla, soaking, small, grand, or whirlpool — take off your shoes, get in, and lie back to be sure it is comfortable. If you're really going to use and soak in the tub every day, it's essential to test it. It should support the back, be long enough, and give gentle support to the head and neck. Are arm supports in the right place? Is it deep enough? It should be big enough for two people. Generally, 72 inches long and 42 inches wide makes a good fit.

Whirlpool

The most versatile and useful length is 5½ feet to 6 feet, which is generally big enough for two people. A variable-speed jetstream is excellent for a massage.

There are now many different kinds of jets – from mini-jets, which can be individually adjusted for comfort, to directional jets, which can direct water exactly where it's needed. If you select a whirlpool tub, be sure that it can be filled fast.

Custom Whirlpool

A bath you love — and that fits your contours — can be fitted with whirlpool jets. It can also have a system that heats and recirculates water in a whirlpool to keep the water at a constant temperature. Then it doesn't have to be refilled constantly to keep the water hot. Remember that an access panel is required for whirlpool servicing. Plan the layout accordingly.

Professional

It's wise for a large-scale remodel — or a complex one — to hire a specialist bathroom designer. They can save more than their professional fees. Designers know the ropes, have connections to showrooms and craftspeople, and know from years of experience which products really work, which hold up best, and which are the best quality for budget redos.

Materials

Cast-iron is the traditional favorite for tubs, but today's acrylic and marble compositions (limestone/resin) are more pliable, thicker, and easy to repair and clean.

OPPOSITE The ample curves of this gracious (new) tub fit perfectly in the angles of this renovated bathroom.

Value

Usually, you get what you pay for with bathroom fixtures and fittings. Expensive faucets are better designed, well-made, and last longer. Labor costs the same whether you buy a cheap fixture or an expensive one. (Fees of $75 an hour for a plumber or electrician are not uncommon.) Select the most appropriate fittings and fixtures of the best quality in the mid-price range if you're on a budget.

Colors

Lighter colors are easier to keep clean. Dark-colored baths and lavatories — black, dark green, dark blue — show water spots and soap spots.

Matching

While it is true that all whites go together, they might not all match. Even pieces from the same design collection might not match up. Acrylic and porcelain whites might not be the same tone. Don't obsess about this — white looks different in changing light. White is still the most perfect color for a bath. Biscuit (palest beige) is also handsome. Remember — color dates fast.

It's Your Bath

Don't think resale. Bathrooms are so personal. It's impossible to know what the next buyer of the house will like. Go with what you love and will use and enjoy. The next buyer may plan to rip it all out and upgrade anyway. He or she may need a different kind of bathroom — with higher countertops, an enclosed shower, a bidet, better lighting.

Toilets

Wall-mounted toilets are beginning to catch on. The flushing mechanism is usually in the wall. Wall-mounted toilets (the newest are in stainless steel) are easy to clean and save floor space. They can be custom-mounted to a comfortable height. (They're also quieter because the tank is in the wall.)

Safety

Install grab bars on the wall beside tubs and whirlpool baths. If you'll be showering in the bathtub, install a slip-proof surface on the bottom.

A B O V E Light waves: Glass blocks were used for this masterful bathroom to bring in light while maintaining privacy. The freestanding counter saves crucial floor space and makes bathroom cleanup quick and easy.

O P P O S I T E This bath is new and adds retro curves to a clean-lined bathroom. Note the hand-held shower. Design: Andree Putman.

Should it be tile, hardwood, limestone, or vinyl? Selecting the appropriate material will save floor problems later.

San Francisco designer/contractor Lou Ann Bauer works with a wide variety of flooring materials – and finds that each has virtues and vices. The vinyl flooring many love to hate is very cost effective and durable, and it won't stain. Stone looks elegant, but the labor costs for installation are often high. Carpet is cushy – but marks easily. Here, Bauer weighs the pros and cons.

VINYL

Pros:

- low cost
- coved edges capture water
- won't stain
- wide range of colors and textures
- tiles can be replaced

Cons:

- limited aesthetic quality – fake stone or terra cotta fools no one
- can look utilitarian, commercial
- can look cheap, too glossy
- tiles may allow water seepage to the subfloor

CERAMIC TILE

Pros:

- waterproof
- enormous range of color, textures, styles, sizes, and patterns
- extremely durable
- easy to maintain
- small areas can be repaired or replaced
- heating can be installed to warm floor

Cons:

- dropped objects can break on the hard surface
- leg fatigue
- grout can wear and discolor
- noisy
- mortar bed can cause height problems on thresholds
- slick, high-gloss tiles are slippery when wet

STONE TILE

Pros:

- classic, elegant look
- extremely durable
- easy to maintain
- can be cut to any size
- natural, warm feel
- can be warmed with subfloor heat

Cons:

- expensive (both material and installation)
- may stain
- noisy
- mortar bed may cause height problems on thresholds
- shiny marble, slick stones can be slippery and dangerous

CONCRETE (TILE AND POURED)

Pros:

- sleek, smooth, hip, industrial look
- can be custom-colored – from solid to variegated
- can be made to look like stone or marble
- cost effective

Cons:

- stains
- noisy
- can be slippery when wet
- can crack at stress joints

WOOD

Pros:

- warm, rich look
- easy on feet and legs
- many variations of grains and colors
- can be custom-colored, painted, stained
- teak is handsome, practical for wet areas
- moderate installation cost

Cons:

- water damage, dry rot, board lift
- must be sealed (satin-finish sealant should be less slippery)

CARPET

Pros:

- low cost, easy to install
- easily changed or replaced
- warm to feet and cozy in winter
- wide variety – flat weaves, sisal weaves are best
- area rugs can warm the room

Cons:

- water damage, rot, mildew
- bleach, solvents, hair color will discolor and mark

carpet permanently
- not waterproof

TERRAZZO

Pros:

- continuous poured surface
- multicolored (custom or stock)
- shells, stones, and other decorative objects can be added to mix
- logos, borders, and designs can be incorporated
- heating can be installed beneath floor

Cons:

- expensive
- requires easy access to the bathroom for pumping in materials
- hard to match for future repair

NONSKID COATINGS (SPRAY-ON APPLICATION)

Pros:

- low cost
- continuous, nonskid
- industrial, clean look
- less fatigue for legs

Cons:

- practical but not especially aesthetic
- difficult to repair small sections
- limited integral color palette

OPPOSITE Heaven is in the details: A faux-stone tile floor, graceful Venetian-style lighting, white linen fabrics. Design: Kate McIntyre and Brad Huntzinger.

OPPOSITE In this renovated San Francisco bathroom designed by Lou Ann Bauer, a Kohler tub takes center stage. The floor is marble. Chair is by Ironies, Oakland.

ABOVE A concrete wall and poured concrete floor create a cool, modern contrast to the antique porcelain sink and tub in Madeleine Corson's and Thomas Heinser's live/work loft.

The counter probably gets the hardest and most consistent use of any surface in the bathroom. But aesthetics are just as important and function. Is glass practical? Will marble stain? Is wood a realistic choice? There's Corian (solid synthetic), along with glass, marble, granite and other stones, wood, concrete, laminates, stainless steel, ceramic tile. Designer/contractor Lou Ann Bauer has helpful advice on sorting out the best, most cost-effective materials.

CERAMIC TILE

Pros:

- waterproof, heatproof
- widest possible selection of colors, textures, patterns, sizes, thicknesses, qualities
- domestic and imported readily available
- small areas can be replaced or repaired
- can be used on small and large surfaces

Cons:

- dropped objects can break on the hard surface
- grout may be hard to clean, and may discolor
- noisy

- mortar bed may cause height problems on vanity tops with drawers

STONE (SLAB AND TILE)

Pros:

- elegant, classic look
- very durable
- can be cut in any size
- beautiful colors; individual, natural patterns
- natural coloring goes with a wide range of styles and decors

Cons:

- high installation cost
- stone can be very expensive
- noisy
- dropped objects may break on the hard surface
- tiles may have grout lines

SOLID SYNTHETIC

Pros:

- continuous, smooth surface, no grout
- coved back edges and rolled front edges offer good water capture
- large selection of colors and patterns
- non-staining, repairable
- sinks may be under-mounted
- edging can vary, and may incorporate other materials
- generally moderately priced

Cons:

- design choice and colors are limited to manufacturer's offerings
- synthetic look
- can burn

- must be installed by a factory-approved dealership

CONCRETE (TILE AND POURED)

Pros:

- modern, industrial look
- custom coloring and tinting
- can be made to look like stone or marble
- cost-effective

Cons:

- stains
- noisy
- can crack at stress joints
- must be professionally installed

WOOD

Pros:

- warm, rich, friendly look
- enormous variety of grains, thicknesses, colors
- can be stained and custom-colored
- teak is excellent for wet surfaces
- moderately expensive, easy to install
- butcherblock, the classic countertop, is durable and easily available
- wide range of choices – from super-fine custom-crafted woods to simple country-looking counters

Cons:

- may look too casual for the city
- board lift, dry rot, or water damage
- can burn or stain

GLASS

Pros:
- medium cost
- many different colors
- can be finished with sandblasting
- can be laminated with other materials between layers
- clean, gleaming look
- easy to clean, hygienic
- water-resistant and waterproof
- temperable
- works with both traditional and modern styles
- sink can be under-mounted

Cons:
- can break or chip
- soap may leave spots

LAMINATES

Pros:
- the most inexpensive countertop
- continuous surface, moldable splash and front edge
- available in the most colors and patterns
- colors can be added to produce a custom look
- can be purchased in prefab lengths – ideal for the do-it-yourselfer

Cons:
- plastic, synthetic look
- patterns are trendy and will become dated (think hula hoops)
- can burn or singe
- sinks must be top-mounted

METALS

Pros:
- heat resistant, will not singe or burn
- continuous sheet surface
- modern, cool, crisp, industrial look
- integral sinks can be built into countertops
- many available varieties – stainless steel, galvanized steel, zinc, copper, tin, brass
- can be fabricated into any style
- custom-grooved drainboards (practical and contemporary looking) can be fabricated

Cons:
- can be expensive
- difficult to repair small sections
- copper may puncture, bend, dent, or scratch
- surprisingly high maintenance – metals scratch and oxidize easily, so must be polished and buffed to maintain gleaming appearance
- can be difficult to find a fabricator and installer

ABOVE Bow-fronted marble counters, nickel-plated fittings. Design: Tucker & Marks.

OPPOSITE A modern, gleaming glass counter. Design: Michael Berman.

FAUCETS & SHOWERHEADS

Today's bathroom fittings can be retro or ultramodern, nickel-plated, brass, porcelain, or chrome.

Bath showrooms, plumbing supply stores, home supply companies, salvage yards, and specialty stores today have dazzling and daunting displays of bathroom faucets, powder room fittings, showerheads, and hand-held showers. Even a small showroom is likely to have hundreds of permutations on the two-handles-and-a-faucet theme. Top bathroom fittings companies — lines such as Waterworks, Kallista, Hansgrohe, Phylrich, and Kohler now offer fittings in shiny-, matte-, or satin-finish nickel, chrome, and brass. Some companies sell 10 or 12 different finishes, from green patina to black, white porcelain, and bronze.

Lori Hom Chiang, San Francisco manager for the Connecticut-based Waterworks company said that it is important to select faucets for function as well as style. "We recommend that our customers look at many different designs before making a final selection," she said. "Ask advice from knowledgeable showroom staff, the contractor, or a bathroom designer. They understand proportions and all the practicalities and will guide you to the best choice." Here, Hom Chiang shares her tips on selecting faucets and showerheads.

Faucet Facts

Size: Faucets and fittings must be appropriate to the scale of the room — big, small — and the size of the washbasin or bath. The proportion of a lavatory set is especially crucial — a complex, large faucet and handles should not in installed in a small, neat powder room washbasin.

Consistency: The fittings should be consistent with the whole bathroom design. Contemporary styles are usually best for clean, modern rooms. More decorative styles (not necessarily traditional) work well with classic or traditional-style rooms. However, there are no absolute rules. Sometimes, the most attractive design can juxtapose an elaborate wall-mounted turn-of-the-century-style nickel tub filler and a hand-held shower with a curvy cradle, with a simple all-white tiled bathroom. Or pure, sleek, sculptural faucets and bath mixers can look elegant in a richly textured bathroom.

Decor: Consider using faucets and handles as the "jewelry" of a bathroom. That doesn't mean that handles are mounted with rose quartz or dressed in glitzy gold-tone finishes or cloisonne, but that the fittings are the best quality, that they are installed perfectly, and that they make the whole bathroom design sing.

Finishes: Nickel, chrome, brass (matte and glossy), and porcelain are the basics — and many manufacturers have dozens of applied finishes. Chrome is the most durable, and it is recommended for outdoor showers. Nickel is now extremely popular because it is rather neutral and has a very warm cast. For cleaning, it's best to use mild liquid soap — no abrasives. Brass will oxidize over time. Some homeowners want that look; others avoid brass because it marks and ages.

OPPOSITE This showerhead is adjustable. Handles are easy for soapy hands to grip. Design: Alice Wiley, Rob Wilkinson.

Variations: Gooseneck spouts are useful for rinsing hair. They're also versatile, as well as decorative. They should have an aerator to diffuse the water flow and minimize splashing.

Matching: Lavatory sets (bathroom faucets), shower heads and valves, and tub fillers, should all match in materials as well as style.

Positioning: The spray of water from the faucet should hit the center or the deepest part of the wash basin. Try the handles and the valves — and be sure that they feel comfortable in the hand. You should be able to get a good grip. It's annoying when slippery, soapy hands slither on faucets. It's important that water can be turned off quickly and easily.

Shower Power

It's twenty private minutes of revival, relaxation, refreshment, and stress-reduction. Showering is the early-morning rite of passage and an end-of-day refuge. Whether for shampooing, muscle-relaxing, speedy rinsing, skin-tingling, shaving, or soaking, the showerhead and hand-held shower must be chosen specifically for its purposes. Products range from purely practical small showerheads and body sprays to decorative porcelain and brass hand-held showers, grand-hotel-sized shower roses, and elaborate combinations of exposed thermostatic valves, shower diverters, gooseneck rigid risers, and brass showerheads with all the elegance of a royal crown. There are sleek, levered handles, wall-mounted faucets, single-lever faucets, even elaborate brass-and-porcelain fittings with the look of hot-and-cold-running-maids-style Edwardian hotel bathrooms.

It's possible to custom-design a system of one or two adjustable showerheads, shower sprays, and sprays that can be programmed to drench, massage, pulsate, and rinse. Outmoded showerheads can be

converted to new, jet-powered pulsating models. Whichever style is selected, it should be the best quality, with ceramic-disc technology and, generally, brass construction.

Temperature: Some new showers have a pressure-balanced thermostatic control — a "temperature memory." The wall-mounted valve is set at the ideal temperature so that you don't have to make adjustments each time the shower is turned on.

Power: Showers can now be fitted with pressure-balancing systems that automatically adjust to changes in water temperature, so that blasts of hot or cold water do not rain down on the shower occupant when a toilet is flushed.

Hand-Held: One of the newest additions to shower fittings is the hand-held shower. There are many choices of styles offered by companies such as Waterworks, Dornbracht, Jado, Phylrich, Czech & Speake, Grohe, and Jacuzzi — including a pulsating head, a fine spray, and heads with up to eight shower patterns. They can be used for shampooing, rinsing, and for washing down the shower or tub. Be sure the grip is weighty and firm — not slippery. Wristblade handles and levers are easiest for use by individuals with physical limitations.

Rain, Rain: Leading companies such as Waterworks and Kallista also offer large 12-inch-diameter shower roses (also called rain showers) the size of pie plates. There's nothing more luxurious at day's end — especially a hot day — than drenching yourself beneath one of these beauties. It's a misconception that rain showers require a large flow of water or great water pressure. They can be used on standard water systems.

Style: The first decision to make is whether to have a concealed or exposed shower system. Exposed shower systems have all the shower valves and fittings mounted on the wall. They can also be concealed in the wall, with only the valves and the head exposed.

Diverters: Ask your plumber about diverters. They're the in-wall mechanisms that control the flow of water from one fitting to another. For example, when the showerhead is switched on, the diverter turns off the hand-held shower. Some bathers prefer a separate on/off valve for each function to provide versatility.

A B O V E Retro-style fittings and accessories make bathing a pleasure. Soap and sponge holders drain well.

O P P O S I T E Think about use, tactile pleasure, and aesthetics: Consider placing the faucet and handles to one side of the bowl.

DEFINITIONS

What's the difference between a fixture and a faucet? Here's help with the lingo.

FIXTURES The larger fixed "furniture" of a bathroom – Toilets, pedestals, bidets, basins, lavatories, sometimes the bathtub.

VANITY Usually the counter and basin with a mirror above.

FAUCET Any style of spout from which water flows. (This does not include the valves or handles.)

FITTINGS Faucets, showerheads, the tub filler (exposed or concealed), body sprays, bidet fittings, hand showers.

ACCESSORIES Robe hooks, towel bars, paper holders, soap dishes, shelves, toothbrush holders, and other amenities.

ENCLOSURE The panels made of glass (or other materials) which surround the shower stall. Many home supply stores sell ready-to-go shower stalls, which are especially useful for budget remodels and bathrooms with a minimum of floor space.

LAVATORY The pedestal sink, the washbasin. (To the trade, a "lav set" is the faucet and two handles threesome.) Generally porcelain or acrylic, but may also be custom-made in marble, various stones, glass, brushed steel, copper, or other metals. It's usually prudent to select a basin in white, ivory, or beige. Colored fixtures can soon become dated-looking, and may quickly show water marks, soap spots, and dabs of toothpaste. Black is especially to be avoided.

SHOWERHEAD Showerheads come in hundreds of styles today, and may be wall-mounted (fixed) or flexible and hand-held. Among the best brands are Speakman and Waterworks. In addition to basic showers that simply spurt water, showerheads may also have ball joints for superior positioning of the water jet, plus adjustable water streams from gentle rain to invigorating needles and pulsating jets of water. New showerheads may also be designed to conserve water. Gaining in popularity are large "rain shower" showerheads (often around 12 inches in diameter) that drench the body in a steady rainfall.

WHIRLPOOL BATH A bath with a motor, designed to direct soothing jets of water. Baths come in hundreds of styles, sizes, shapes.

ABOVE A broad counter and neatly proportioned faucet give this bathroom a clean, straightforward utility.

OPPOSITE A large shower and bath with a view, and a sauna, left. Design: John Fortney.

THE JOYS OF SALVAGING

Vintage bathroom fixtures, etched-glass shades, and creaky old fittings add charm and grace to renovated bathrooms.

Homeowners, architects, and designers have been heading to the finest salvage companies to clamber among piles of dusty ceramic fixtures in search of old cast-iron baths, eccentric lighting, hand-painted tiles, thirties pedestals and washbasins, ziggurats of iron fences, and turn-of-the-century architectural details. These handsome and highly individual pieces bestow character and quirkiness to a bathroom — and exude the quality and hands-on craftsmanship of long ago.

Starting out, it's a good idea to make a survey of a few salvage yards. Some are little more than junk yards, a few steps above a town dump. Many simply sell anything that comes their way. A weekend reconnoiter of salvage yards reveals that some of what is available is strange and wonderful, while much is not distinguished, merely old. But often, it's in those boneyards — among the harvest-gold fifties pedestals and sixties aqua or maroon toilets — where the best bargains can be found. Persistence and frequent visits will usually pay off with handsome wrought-iron etageres, serpentine faucets, delicate iron curtain rods, or odd cuts of rare stone and stacks of old tiles in appealingly unfashionable hues. Barging backstage at a marble company may yield broken and oddly shaped pieces of marble and slabs of granite, even broken statuary. Jumbled in a corner may be unfinished pieces of stone, oxidized brass fittings, and odds and ends of marble that could be used decoratively or as pieces of mosaic on a new floor.

The best salvage yards (like Ohmega Salvage and Omega Too in Berkeley, California, and companies in Chicago, New Orleans, and New York) offer an ever-changing display of carefully edited, fine-quality old lighting in a wide range of styles. It's in those highly competitive markets that the choicest baths, pedestals, architectural findings, and marble will turn up. Generally, the lighting will have been rewired and repaired, fixtures will have been cleaned, and lost

parts replaced. Jana and Steve Drobinsky, owners of Berkeley's revered Ohmega Salvage (started more than 24 years ago by a hippie commune), are experts at finding and fixing vintage household goods. They search around the country for top-quality stuff. Visits to their site are like a treasure hunt, and the truly dedicated will unearth etched-glass mirrors, exquisite lighting, convent furniture, hygienic hospital equipment, or glass door handles.

"Some people turn to salvage to save money and to get something with unusual character," said Jana. "Many people love the fact that old bathroom equipment was built sturdier and heavier — like a battleship. It's reassuring to find a 90-year-old cast-iron bath or a 70-year-old sink in great condition.

ABOVE This renovated Victorian bathroom was "updated" with quirky faucets and memorabilia. Design: Lou Ann Bauer.

OPPOSITE Vintage light fittings (rewired and repaired) complement handpainted wall tiles. Design: Doug Biederbeck.

Others want lighting or accessories that ooze nostalgia. What could be nicer than washing your hands in a washbasin that reminds you of your grandmother's house?" Everything in the bathroom does not have to be old. A pair of old sconces, an old mirror, or a counter of old marble may be all it takes to give an all-white bathroom a retro look. Here, the Drobinskys offer their advice.

Cost

Many home renovators first turned to salvage yards because old sinks and faucets were cheaper. Treasures-for-less are to be found. For a do-it-yourselfer, an old washstand, marble slabs, brass fittings, or a discarded bath can be a bargain. Since salvage became chic, demand has increased and prices have risen. Now, beautiful old brass fittings and rare vintage lights are often more expensive than new ones. Old cast-iron baths may need refinishing and as a result will cost more than basic new baths. Often, installing old washstands or claw-foot tubs may require expensive labor, especially if plumbing has to be moved or adjusted. Still, salvage-yard searches can turn up highly individual and one-of-a-kind bathroom accessories or fittings that add pleasure to the daily bath.

Character

Most salvage-lovers are looking for treasure — fittings

ABOVE Artful craftsmanship gives this bathroom a retro air. Inspiration: Antique Japanese cabinetry.

OPPOSITE Isn't it romantic: Floral fabric and handpainted flowers on the tub make this bathroom festive.

and fixtures with details that could not be duplicated today. Elaborate porcelain fixtures and elaborate shower attachments have their own odd charm. (Note, however, that leading companies such as Waterworks are now reproducing those venerable English and European fittings and fixtures.)

Labor

Some tradespeople do not have the expertise or patience to repair and install old fixtures. It may be best to check with a contractor or tradesperson before purchasing a bath, cranky old faucets, a grand hotel-sized washstand with chrome legs, or a theatrical vintage light fixture. Good salvage yards will most likely have a list of recommended tradespeople who can adjust the innards and workings of plumbing fixtures and lights.

Toilets

It is now almost impossible to install a salvage toilet in a new bathroom legally. Most codes require a low-flow toilet. A historic home restoration may allow an old toilet to be replaced. The best solution is to find a new (low-flow) toilet with a retro look.

Handles and Faucets

It used to be standard to have separate hot and cold handles. They can be installed in new washstands or counters — but the holes may need to be enlarged. Putting new faucets in old sinks may also require some adjustment. Check carefully before purchasing.

Tiles

Old hand-finished tiles usually come in small batches, and can be used decoratively as an accent for plain white tiles. Mismatched Arts & Crafts and hand-painted feature tiles can be used as a backsplash, as a band of color behind a bath, or along the top of a wainscot.

Light Fixtures

They can sometimes be purchased as is, but it is best to buy them ready to go and ready to install. They often have eccentric styles and more detail than new lights. Look for old frosted glass, amber, clear, and etched-glass shades, old brass fixtures, nickel-plated, and Craftsman-style lights. Old sconces and ceiling lights add to the ambience of an old bathroom. Note that vintage fixtures don't all have to match – in fact, they look more interesting if they don't.

Accessories

These are often hard to find — they were usually discarded. Brass towel bars with nickel plating, old wall-mounted soap dishes, bath-side sponge holders, towel

racks, glass holders, small glass shelves with brass brackets, and porcelain shelves are all very desirable. It might be a good idea to advise the salvage yard owners that these are a priority — and have them saved for you when they turn up.

Architectural Fragments

Corbels, brackets, ceiling rosettes, old marble slabs, marble brackets and window frames, mirrors, and wainscot can all add great charm to a new bathroom. Broken marble pieces can be used to make a mosaic floor — or a mosaic backsplash.

Mirrors

Mottled old mirrors in good old frames may be odd shapes — and their arches and odd angles make a room more intriguing. The best mirrors have beveled edges.

Caveat Emptor

Old fixtures and architectural fragments may have come from many different parts of the country. Changes in plumbing and lighting codes should be checked — perhaps in a chat with a licensed plumber, electrician, or contractor.

Word to the Wise

Before leaving the yard or store with trophies being purchased "as is," double check to see if there are any parts missing or broken, or if there is any sort of guarantee. Replacement parts are often impossible to find. Even if the pedestal is cheap and the sconces are a bargain, it's best to know that they could be returned or exchanged.

LEFT Faucets may be framed with vintage plaster gargoyles. Powder rooms can be playful. Design: Lou Ann Bauer.

OPPOSITE Grand hotel: Retro-style fixtures may be vintage — or created to look old. Design: Michael Berman.

LET THERE BE LIGHT

Bathrooms can be romantic, cheerful, clinical, soothing, and refreshing — it all depends on good lighting.

The key to planning good bathroom lighting is to layer lighting so that it is bright enough to illuminate the whole room and the mirror without glare. A bright light shining down from above the mirror will have a harsh, ghoulish effect and is not recommended. For a decorative "dressing room" look that's also ideal for shaving or applying makeup, three or four strips of 15- to 40-watt white "G" bulbs can be installed on each side of the mirror. These will also provide balanced lighting with few shadows. Caprice De Beaux Carter, a lighting consultant at Limn Company in San Francisco, shares some lighting pointers.

Saving Energy

California's Title 24 energy-efficiency regulation (like those of other states) requires that the first bathroom light source switched on must be fluorescent. Many new fluorescent tubes cast flattering light. It is possible to light the bathroom with recessed fluorescents.

Vanity

The most important bathroom lighting is at the vanity. Sconces, pendant fixtures, vintage glass-shaded lamps, or a strip of lights on each side of the mirror will give the most pleasing light. Wattage will depend on the size of the bathroom. If the light must go above the mirror, the most ideal illumination is a fixture such as "Robbia Full" by Artemide, which has two 100-watt lamps installed behind a hand-blown milk-glass diffuser.

Overall Lighting

While a large bathroom may need a central ceiling fixture for overall lighting, ceiling lighting as the only source of light is generally inefficient and unflattering.

Dimmers

Dimmer controls on all lights will make fine-tuning mood lighting possible. If you love to lower light levels for long, quiet soaks in the tub, dimmer controls are essential.

Variations

Table lamps on one or both sides of the vanity, or on a small table near the bath, are an attractive and versatile way to light a bathroom. They can provide pleasing "pools" of light as an alternative to ambient lighting and cast a glow on collections of silver brushes and combs or on a basket of shells. Adjustable table lamps are useful lighting for reading in the bath.

Not Recommended

Track lighting, harsh vanity lighting, and extremely bright lights are not recommended in a bathroom.

A B O V E Neat wall sconces, mounted high, cast even light and are very easy to keep clean. Note the practical recessed lighting.

O P P O S I T E Light work: Old textured-glass panes create artful tonal variations in this custom-made window. Design: Daren Joy.

Accent lights may be useful for lighting art or for high-lighting an architectural feature, but they should not be used at a mirror.

Safety

For children or houseguests unfamiliar with the house, install a night-light in an outlet near the floor so that the bathroom is illuminated at night. In the winter, in the country or in remote areas where power failures are not unknown, keep a flash-light or a fluorescent utility light in a bathroom cabinet for emergency lighting. (And don't forget matches for candles.)

Romantic

Nothing can set a romantic and relaxing mood at night faster than natural beeswax candles, or lightly scented ivory-colored candles. Stand them in old sil-ver or crystal candlesticks. Beeswax pillar candles posed on small round glass holders will burn for hours. Votive candles in small glass holders can stand along a window ledge, along the wall beside the bath, or on a small table next to the bath.

OPPOSITE Variable lighting for this renovated bathroom was designed with a flourish. Design: Osburn Design, San Francisco.

BELOW Pairs of elegant counter lamps (for incandescent or candlelight) are effective here. Design: Tucker & Marks, San Francisco.

ABOVE Wall sconces illuminate with poetry and special style. An arched window, quirky antiques, a bold framed mirror, and a handsome custom-made counter make the simple act of hand-washing a memorable moment.

OPPOSITE Luminous details count: Careful selection of lighting is crucial in bathrooms. It illuminates tasks, makes people using the bathroom look attractive, and adds style to the room. Here, a subtle curved sconce casts light over the bath – but does not protrude to catch unwary heads.

CHILDREN'S BATHROOMS

Kids and bath time are a wonderful combination.
Cecilia Campa, designer and mother of two, has great advice.

"Don't be in a hurry to bathe your infant in the tub," advised Cecilia Campa, who lives in San Francisco. "Babies who cannot sit up confidently should not be bathed there. They require strong balancing skills to be able to maneuver a tub. A slip or a loss of balance can undermine their confidence and cause 'bath fears.'"

Use the Sink

The kitchen sink is a great place to bathe a baby up to six months old. The height and stability make it especially safe and easy to handle a lovely slippery baby. And it's possible to keep sponges and gentle shampoos and towels on the counter close by. Place a towel beneath the baby to prevent slipping and sliding, and another towel between the baby's back and the sink. Kohler makes a perfect sink for washing both babies and dishes (Model K5989). A portion of this sink is rounded and not too close to the faucets and water controls.

Mats

When the child is old enough — and secure enough — to sit alone in a bathtub, purchase a nonslip bath mat for the bottom of the tub. Some mats come equipped with temperature sensor devices that indicate when the water is too hot for baby. Do not leave a baby unattended in the tub. Stay and play.

Colors

It is best to avoid decorating the children's bathroom in primary colors. Hard yellows and reds and strong blues are perfect for baby toys but not for a bathroom.

Decor

Children grow up fast and as teenagers will not appreciate the ducks, frogs, and dinosaurs on tiles or a mural that made bathtime fun when they were small. The key to maximizing the investment in a bathroom remodel is longevity and versatility. Choose timeless design approaches and materials (like marble, stone, plain tiles) that focus less on entertainment value or "cute" themes. Consider using texture (mosaics, relief tiles, undulating tiles, sandblasted surfaces) and timeless colors (cream, palest greens, soft whites, pale aquatic blues). Another way to add interest to a secondary bathroom is with sculptural shapes (a handsome faucet, an interesting mirror).

Shower

A shower stall is not essential for a children's bathroom. Stub it out on the wall above the tub for future use, but hold off on installing glass shower doors around the tub. It is easier to bathe the baby

---

ABOVE Cheery color and classic patterning strike a happy note. Note the generous pedestal sink.

OPPOSITE Child's play: With white tiles, curved surfaces, and ample space, children can cavort and moms and dads don't have to worry. Color accents should be subtle.

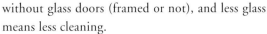

without glass doors (framed or not), and less glass means less cleaning.

Safety

Children love to play with water, so to prevent painful bumps and bruises, cover the water spout with a special soft cover (from a hardware store).

Floor

Children's bathroom floors are often (always!) wet — and children are always in a hurry. If using tiles, choose non-slip or textured tiles for the floor — crisscross raised patterns or undulating designs — to prevent slipping.

Storage

Children need a lot of closet space for bath towels, special shampoos, step stools, and bath toys. Plan extra storage, if possible, with adjustable shelves.

As the years pass, children's needs change and the dozens of small towels needed for baby are swapped for big bath sheets. Provide lots of hooks, racks, and bars for hanging towels, robes, and face cloths, so that children can get in the habit of picking them up and letting them dry.

Best of all, take a bath with the baby. Add gentle bubble bath, rubber duckies, toy submarines, some play fish, and a bubble blower so that you can play together. Baby's hair gets clean, everyone's relaxed, and both baby and parents will sleep especially well.

ABOVE RIGHT Mixing old and new – a rattan chair, bright new fixtures, an antique table – makes this bathroom personal.

ABOVE LEFT Whimsical animal knobs and a spigot for purified water are practical, decorative notes in this child's bathroom. Design: Lou Ann Bauer.

OPPOSITE Simple grace notes – a zigzag of tiles, fresh air, a curly wall sconce – take this bathroom out of the ordinary.

THE POWDER ROOM

This small room may be used by guests and family only occasionally, but the design deserves careful consideration.

Small guest bathrooms — usually called powder rooms — aren't subjected to the kind of rough-and-tumble day-to-day wear meted out to other bathrooms. No one actually bathes there. No one showers there. In fact, guests spend just a few minutes freshening up, primping, checking makeup, and straightening ties before heading back to the dinner table or the cocktail party.

"I always tell my clients that they should not be stingy with mirrors in a powder room," said San Francisco designer Michael Tedrick. "A sweet little mirror looks nice, but it doesn't serve any purpose. If a full-length mirror can fit, guests and family can use it to check their sartorial perfection."

Lighting

Sconces or brackets on each side of the mirror work best. Line silk shades with shell pink silk for the most flattering glow. Overhead lighting, whether from the ceiling or above the mirror, is the least attractive. Fluorescent lighting is generally not welcoming or attractive in this small room.

Faucets

The water should run directly into the center of the bowl so that it does not splash on to a guest's clothing.

Bowl

The best washbasin height for hand washing is approximately 32 inches. Some like it higher, but 32 inches is a good compromise for both tall and petite guests.

Floors

Bare floors (hardwood, honed stone, tile) are best. Carpet should not be fitted unless the room is generous, with a separate enclosed toilet. Avoid rugs — guests may slip on them.

Natural Light

If the powder room is carved out during a re-model, consider putting in a small window. It's nice to be able to open a win-dow and have a sense of the outdoors. A tailored curtain can add privacy and a decorating flourish.

Door

A pocket door will not feel private — or seem soundproof. The door should have a secure lock that is quick, easy, and quiet to operate.

Fan

Don't scrimp on the obligatory fan. It should not be a budget-saver or an afterthought, nor sound like a Bugatti at the start of a road race. Get the quietest and the most efficient.

ABOVE Indigo glow: Even a small powder room can be dressed with cheer. Blue tones add unity and verve here.

OPPOSITE Mirror image: A small washbasin, curved counter — and a small antique lamp — have the graciousness of a larger room.

Art

This room should be functional and comfortable, but it is not the place for major art.

Hooks

Install small double robe hooks to hold jewelry or a watch. Mount them close to the lavatory to be used while guests rinse their hands. A small chair on which to place a jacket or handbag is useful.

Guest Towels

A basket of small linen hand towels is a thoughtful gesture. For less formal occasions, top-quality, fabric-like white paper towels are ideal. Provide a small basket on the floor for their disposal.

Soap

Provide a small basket or bowl of unwrapped white lightly scented single-use soaps. (Aggressively scented potpourri is not necessary.)

Flowers

Don't overdo floral arrangements. Orchids are perhaps a touch formal. A few garden flowers or grasses in a simple vase are perfectly adequate for this brief encounter.

OPPOSITE Attention to detail: Framed prints, sculptures, an antique chair and handsome tiles entertain the eye. Design: Henry Johnstone & Co., Pasadena.

BELOW The best place for soaps, bath salts, shampoos: In vintage glass containers. They're decorative, practical.

AMENITIES

The bathroom should be well-supplied with essentials — pretty soaps, shower caps, slippers, easy-to-read scales, natural sponges, big robes.

STAY WARM A wall-mounted towel-warmer is one of the hot new bathroom requirements. It can warm the room, too.

MIRRORS An adjustable swivel mirror with an extendable arm can be used both at the washbasin and in the bath.

SHOWERS Frameless shower doors are usually the most aesthetic choice. If a shower curtain is necessary, make it plain white terry cloth backed with clear or matte white vinyl.

EXTRAS Antique accessories, a silver baby cup for cotton swabs, a handsome English boar-bristle shaving brush, boxes of extra blades, French handmade "tortoiseshell" hair combs, Scandinavian toothpaste, Bulgari Eau Parfumee, and other entertaining extras make mundane daily tasks more interesting.

HOOKS There's never a place to hang wet towels and damp robes! Add ornamental hooks on the backs of doors, on cabinet doors, on the wall. Attach them high. Big vintage hooks are especially effective.

ABOVE Orchids (in cachepots) love bathrooms and thrive in the steamy atmosphere.

OPPOSITE This Southern California bathroom was designed for two people who love clean lines and lots of light. Note that the stone wall affords privacy — and acts as a handsome piece of sculpture.

DESIGN THAT LASTS

Avoid bathrooms trends or fads. Today's styles can look dated in a year or two. How do you avoid being a fashion victim?

Designing in a classic mode affords a wide catalogue of styles. Timeless design can have an Arts & Crafts balance (see opposite page) or look rigorous (photograph at right), but it should never be trite. It is essential to read books on a range of period styles, and to visit cabinetmakers, tile showrooms, and bathroom specialists to feast on all the possibilities.

No Whims

Avoid flavor-of-the-month accessories and decor. Color combinations that are "hot" one season will soon look old-hat. (Remember avocado, aqua and harvest gold?)

Avoid Period Style

Stay away from one-note design such as Art Deco, Shaker, Mission, or Victorian unless you are an expert and a purist through and through (and only if the architecture supports the look). It's difficult to give period and vintage bathrooms the correct scale, style, and tone. Similarly, re-creating Nantucket, Cape Cod, or Connecticut in California can lead to a sense of dislocation, with the Pacific Ocean and palm trees out the window. "Authentic" museum-like rooms give no room for personal expression or updating. Follow your own design ideas. It is usually an individual and unpredictable approach that gives a room allure.

Mix Old and New

Mix antiques and vintage furniture with contemporary prints. Everything in a room should not be new.

Windows

Fancy, fussy draperies are not appropriate. Keep the look tailored, simple, unpretentious — and easy to clean. A synthetic basket-weave mesh shade is unaffected by moisture, lets in some light, and looks neat.

Quality Lasts

Insist on the best-quality tiles and flooring materials, window coverings, and the most careful craftsmanship you can afford.

Eclectic

Designing rooms with an eclectic spirit gives you the freedom to change and improve them — without having to start over from scratch. Move any wall-mounted photographs and furniture around and rearrange accessories from time to time. Don't let the room look like a stage set.

Comfort

Choose classic, straightforward chairs, benches, or ottomans with simple silhouettes. They can easily be recovered and restyled with updated fabrics, whereas elaborate upholstery resists real updating.

ABOVE Steel, glass, and wood come together beautifully here in a simple, symmetrical counter. (See page 82.)

OPPOSITE Superb craftsmanship never goes out of style. Note the varied wood tones, balanced proportions. Design: Lou Ann Bauer.

Walls

Patterned wallpaper looks tired over time. If you want lasting texture or pattern on your walls, look for a paper with a neutral all-over design — or take a class in paint finishes and add small dots, a ribbon stripe, or ragging.

Avoid Loud Fabrics

Don't design your room around one new, bold-patterned fabric or a tricky mix of patterns. Not only will you tire of the patterns quickly, but they restrict possibilities for changing and updating the room.

Symmetry

Bathrooms with symmetrical rhyme and reason — balanced proportions and logical geometries — always feel comfortable and never go out of style. Wise and pleasing symmetry may begin with the square — square floor tiles, a square mirror, a square window, a square countertop, even quirky square drawer pulls. Symmetry may also be maintained with beautiful, sensual curves — a bowed countertop, a round or oval mirror, a luxurious and welcoming oval or round bath. Too many odd, jutting angles in a bathroom can be disconcerting and ungainly and even unsafe.

OPPOSITE Creating simple partitions within a bathroom gives a sense of privacy. Note the generous twin sinks. Architect: Heidi Richardson, San Francisco

BELOW Water world: This Southern California dream bathroom offers the highly rejuvenating luxury of bathing indoors – before taking a plunge outdoors. Design: Nick Berman.

OPPOSITE Double vision: More and more new bathrooms today are being planned with twin exposed sinks and broad, useful counters. Note towels bars.

ABOVE Los Angeles designer Michael Berman designed a generous dressing table with special makeup drawers.

FINE-TUNING A BATHROOM

Today's baths should offer the luxury of peace and visual pleasure.
Dream bathrooms are both beautiful and practical.

Los Angeles-based interior designer Kate Stamps obsesses about interior design details for her clients, so it's not surprising that she would give bathrooms a great deal of thought. She and her architect husband, Odom Stamps, recently moved to a charming 1904 house in Pasadena that they are currently remodeling. "Our bathroom has a lovely private view of the garden through French doors that open out onto a covered porch," said Kate. "It sounds romantic, and it often is. But we also bathe our dogs in the big clawfoot tub, one my husband saved from demolition when he was eight years old." The Stampses' bathroom has many of her ideal features — a large pedestal sink, an oversized water heater, white hexagonal tiles on the floor, and beadboard walls.

Kate Stamps likes the idea of furnishing a great bathroom like a living room, with antiques (not precious) and handsome candlesticks. She likes a comfortable chair, a bookcase where she keeps her favorite books (in paperback). And she believes that the best bathrooms have a balcony or private enclosed terrace with garden vistas. Here, Kate shares her thoughts on the perfect bathroom.

Flowers

It is always a delight to have fresh flowers in the bathroom. (Never dried arrangements, which always look dead and dull and contribute nothing.) Garden flowers such as Paul Neyron roses, mignonette, honeysuckle, lily of the valley, and gardenias fill the air with scent. Daffodils and jonquils are cheerful and refreshing in the spring.

Refreshment

Plan ahead. If a cup of tea is an essential part of the nightly bathing experience, it's a special treat to keep the necessary things to make tea in a nearby closet.

Comfort

The room's temperature must be comfortable year-round. A bathroom must have fast heating and cooling, a powerful fan and exhaust system, and a separate steam room if showers will be hot and steamy enough to peel the wallpaper of the wall. Many architects now install in-floor heating for warmth.

Music

Some people love the company of television programs while they bathe. Checking morning news or stock market reports can become a habit. Kate Stamps prefers a stereo system so that she can listen to NPR's *Morning Edition* as the day begins and Bach's Sonata in D Major as she prepares for bed.

Water Closet

The toilet should have a separate enclosure, perhaps adjacent to the bathroom.

Towels

They should be white, perhaps cream — no trendy colors. There are now many excellent varieties of Egyptian cotton towels, soft and fluffy. Monograms are hand-

---

OPPOSITE Nothing could be cozier: Many homeowners fear that white will look "clinical." Wood and tiles here are creamy white – and could not be friendlier.

some, especially in pale French blue, but they should not be too elaborate. Having dozens of face towels and hand towels stacked neatly in the linen closet is very luxurious.

Practicalities

Laundry chutes are essential. Damp towels, gardening clothes, and old socks should be dispatched immediately. A fine French Brot magnifying mirror with its own illumination is a good investment — anyone who wears makeup will appreciate one. And it's essential to have plenty of outlets for the hair dryer, shaver, curlers, and Water Pic.

Storage

Before planning closets, it's judicious to estimate the number of towels and other things that end up in the bathroom — and double the estimated storage needed. It's better to have too much. Special compartments for shampoos, toothpaste, lotions, razors, medicines, and soap supplies will keep shelves in order.

Privacy

The door should close securely — and lock from the inside if several members of the family will be sharing the room. It should have a solid, well-built door, so that bathers can dream and relax, undisturbed by household sounds. When soaking in the tub, it's nice to spend moments in peace.

OPPOSITE Towels should always be kept at hand and within easy reach of those using the washbasin.

BELOW Storage aplenty: Each cabinet in this bathroom is equipped with ample storage, and the center island has rails for towels.

LINEN CLOSET POINTERS

The well-stocked linen closet. You can never have too many big white towels.

BATH TOWELS Generously sized white or cream bath towels are the most versatile. They're perfect for wrapping just-bathed youngsters, and ideal for in-a-hurry adults. Unbleached natural cotton towels or plain white towels with simple monograms or scalloped edges are classics. Scalloped edges or trim may be in classic dark blue, pink, ivory, or white. Avoid towels in ultrabright or dark colors (except for children) – they generally fade over time. Fashion hues, too, and seasonal colors or patterns generally look as if you're trying too hard. They're towels – not decor.

HAND TOWELS Forget those fingertip towels. No one ever uses them. Look for heavy-weight hotel-style linen hand towels instead. But do have lots of face cloths for bathing.

FLOOR Thick terry-cloth bath mats can be washed easily. Avoid rubberized or overly shaggy mats. Mats that coordinate with towels and other accessories also look like too much attention was paid to functional things.

HOOKS Install large hooks on the back of the door for big, white, spa-like robes.

FRAGRANCE Lavender sachets, soaps, and scented drawer linings keep both stacks of linens and the closet smelling fresh. Avoid strong perfumes.

ABOVE It is essential to have wall hooks or rails for wet towels.

OPPOSITE Shelves make neat, decorative use of wall space.

ESSENTIALS OF GOOD BATHROOM DESIGN

**The best architects and bathroom designers fine-tune materials,
layouts, and floor plans until they are squeaky clean.**

Los Angeles architects Raun Thorp and Brian Tichenor, of Tichenor & Thorp Architects, are known for their updated classic approach to interiors and the elegant finish of their work. They recently bought a house near Beverly Hills and are currently working on renovating it. Bathroom redesign is on their minds.

Materials

The architecture of the house — and the budget — will dictate what's appropriate, said Thorp. Honed marble, matte-glazed or glazed tile are classics. Small white ceramic mosaic tiles (square or hexagonal) in a matte finish can be bordered with a classic Greek key design or a black stripe. Thorp also likes floors of teak and mahogany, traditionally used for ship decks, but the woods must be sealed and cared for. A teak floor would look beautiful in an Asian-style bathroom with a soaking tub.

Wise Money

Thorp recommends first putting money into the finest materials and quality fixtures and fittings instead of whizzbang appliances or a sound system. Faucets, which you touch every day, should be sturdy and practical. It does not make sense, she said, to buy cheap faucets.

Amenities

A seat or footrest in the shower is useful and gives the shower cabinet a more gracious feeling. (This surface may double as a handy shelf.)

Access

If privacy is not an issue, French doors to a garden or to an enclosed terrace can give a bathroom a sense of airiness and light. Even doors opening to a small balcony will double the apparent space of the room and bring sunlight pouring in.

Baths and Whirlpools

Whirlpools and large baths require a lot of hot water. Don't get a whirlpool unless there's a large supply. Oval and rectangular tubs are best. Exaggerated acrylic bath shapes and molded whirlpool shapes with an excess of armrests, footrests, grab bars, and headrests look too elaborate and overdone. Simple silhouettes are better. And if you can create a niche or an archway for the bath, it will add a sense of comfort and enclosure for the bather.

Comfort

The niche for soaps and shampoos should be generous — and should not accumulate water. Shower controls should not be beneath the showerhead — they

ABOVE Counters, surfaces: When planning a new bathroom, it is essential to include broad surfaces for storage, display, mirrors, combs, toiletries.

OPPOSITE The broad surround of this bath makes it easy to access and exit. And there's space for flowers, books, soaps, towels.

should be easily accessible at one side, out of the range of water coming from the showerhead.

Safety

Avoid sunken tubs (on the same level as the floor). They look luxurious to some, and seem modern and sleek, but they are very unsafe. They're hard to get out of, very hard to clean, and get cold easily. Mount the tub or whirlpool so that it is easily accessible — and easy to get out of with the help of wall-mounted grab bars.

Details, Details

In the transition from a marble or tile bathroom floor to a carpeted hallway, inset a level threshold material such as an eight-inch slab of marble or stone cut in the appropriate shape for the doorway. This "finishes" the floor design, and makes the transition less awkward.

Style

Box cabinets beneath sinks (also known as Pullmans) tend to look boxy, take up a lot of space, and are not especially efficient for storage. Instead, build an elegant, broad vanity or clear the decks entirely and install a pedestal sink. For added storage, build a larger, deeper medicine cabinet. A wall-hung cabinet above the toilet can be useful.

The best bathrooms today have low-key elegance; they're not harshly colored or glitzy. The design and facilities must enhance daily life: add bevels to mirrors, perhaps build a dressing table with one-of-a-kind drawer pulls, or invest in a sauna, a whirlpool tub, or an open shower.

ABOVE Tiles set in an imaginative pattern give this small bathroom a kinetic charm. Note the deep window reveal.

OPPOSITE Practicality aside, bathrooms can be full-tilt and very decorative with portraits, elaborate lamps, wallpaper. Design: Joe Ruggiero.

ABOVE In Sonoma County, Suzanne Tucker designed a spacious bathroom with a deep tub, towel shelves, luxurious marble – and an expansive view of a private garden.

OPPOSITE Stripe it up: Broad painted stripes give this narrow corner a sense of dimension and importance. Stripes, unlike patterns, are an eternal design theme and will not date. Note the friendly, sculpted shape of the counter.

SMALL BATHROOMS

**Many houses and apartments are stuck with small bathrooms.
Here's how to turn petite into poetic.**

"Small bathrooms can be very practical and have lots of charm," said San Francisco designer Cecilia Campa. "You just have to pay attention to every little detail. And don't forget the one great advantage to small bathrooms — there's less to clean."

Campa advises against using too many colors in small bathroom design. "Keep colors simple, understated, and cohesive," she suggested. "Simple tone-on-tone white and cream, or very neutral beiges with biscuit are soothing to the eye. If you want a little more pizzazz, use textured tiles, marble, and other stones, or use a little color very sparingly."

Architecture

Take advantage of and emphasize any architectural details available. Wainscotting, crown molding, panelled doors, coved or angled ceilings, even interesting wall paneling or baseboards can give the rooms more distinction.

If the room doesn't offer much, add moldings and a wainscot (even a painted wainscot) and put in a very architectural mirror, tailored draperies, or bolder framing for the window.

Height

Today's idea is to raise the height of the vanity counter from 32 inches to 34 or even 36 inches to avoid back strain. It can maximize space in a small bath, especially if the counter is wall-mounted or mounted on a simple pedestal. However, if children will be using the bathroom, it is not ideal for them. They will require a step stool to reach the counter to brush teeth or wash hands. Select a well-balanced stool with rubber "feet" that won't slide.

No Big Themes

Small bathrooms should not be theme-arama. Every detail, image, or color has more presence in a small bathroom. The sailboats and shells and wavy patterns can become tiresome over time and with close proximity.

Double Sinks

If two washbasins can practically be squeezed in, it is a plus during morning rush hour. But double sinks are not an absolute requirement when space is tight. It's best to have more countertop space than trying to squeeze in an extra sink. A bigger countertop will also make the room seem larger.

Electrical

It is a mistake to have the bathroom exhaust fan turned on with the ceiling light. Put them on separate switches so that they can be controlled and used at different times. In a small bathroom, a silent fan is

ABOVE Tiny and practical: Drawers are tucked under the counter. Note: decorative recessed lighting.

OPPOSITE Imaginative: This marble counter was carefully carved into an awkward corner. Wall-mounted faucets conserve space.

very important. As for lighting, note that some cities require fluorescent lighting to meet energy-saving requirements.

Smooth

In a tight space, it is best to round off countertops and smooth off any surfaces you may be bumping into. Shower door handles, if any, should be flush with the door. Put towel bars and robe hooks where they won't collide with your body.

Space Savers

If it is not possible to fit a tub in the bathroom, fit a shower into a corner. A corner shower stall must be three feet square, minimum, but for most people that provides enough elbow room.

Storage

Look for new storage possibilities. If you have a vanity, add generous drawers and added roll-outs where possible. Recess cabinets and storage niches between the studs in the walls. Use the back of the door for mounting towel bars. Place a towel rack above the bath, and perhaps at one side of the shower away from the spray. Install wall shelves above the counter, and install a small cabinet out of the way on a wall to hold toiletries, hand towels, brushes.

OPPOSITE   To make this bathrooms seem larger, the glass shower enclosure has an angled door. Glass blocks pull light into the room. Note decorative tile detail. Design: Lou Ann Bauer, San Francisco.

BELOW   The stone counter is neatly shaped so it does not jut out into the room. There's generous space here for towels and toiletries.

COLOR SCHEMES

White is increasingly the "color" of choice, but subtle colors used judiciously set styles and moods of a bathroom.

Whether the room is pure, pristine white or the muted color of a Tuscan afternoon, color selection should be precise, judicious, and informed. Any color — even a narrow line of celadon tiles, a shot of sienna or ocher in a pale stone tile, a zigzag of veining in marble, an ivory molding, or a biscuit-colored tub — will have a great impact.

Color designers Jill Pilaroscia and Emily Keenan of Colour Studio Inc. in San Francisco are bold and adventurous with hues and combinations of color. But they're cautious about color in bathrooms. They recommend developing a cohesive, pleasing palette rather than following this-minute trends. "Even a minimally narcissistic individual will glance in the bathroom mirror to check appearances, so color and light must be pleasing, luscious, and inspiring," said Pilaroscia.

White

There are many variations and tonalities of white. Test a few chips or different "swatches" of white paint on a wall before making the big commitment. Check the various tones in all lights — even candlelight. Some whites are cold and blue. Others look drab and gray. Some go very yellow in the sunshine. And white can even have a warm pink glow. All whites do go together — but if you have ultrawhite shiny tiles on the floor or the wainscot, it's probably best to keep the white walls close in tone — not pale blue/white or greenish or cream. Similarly, off-white should be tested for contrast, tones, depth, and effect. If white walls seem too plain, it may be advisable to move up a

notch in hue to bone, ivory, pale sienna, or cream. A French wash — a subtle mottled painted effect — in pale ivory can look subtle and give the effect of (more expensive) glazing.

To Gloss or Not

The most appropriate paints for bathroom walls are most likely semi-gloss or satin finish. Glossy white looks crisp and clean on baseboards and other trim but is too shiny and reflective for expanses of walls. A satin finish on wainscoting, or on the back of a door, or on the bath surround, is more practical than hard-edged gloss.

Flattering

Lighting and colors in the bathroom should enhance the appearance. Mirror reflections should make everyone using the bathroom look attractive, alert, and healthy. Red, blue, and especially green (even pale sage) can cast an odd glow on a naked body. Expanses of colors like celery, burgundy, green, and dark

A B O V E   The joys of bathing, the art of tiles: If you love color, use it judiciously and with verve. Here, cheer for an early morning shower.

O P P O S I T E   Bathrooms should not, generally, be a riot of color. Here, subtle jade-tone tiles and towels enliven an all-white room.

Warm white and a subtle pink/bone color will also brighten a chilly bathroom. Gray/taupe and blue/green colors will probably look drab or chilly.

Paint Effects

Many bathrooms can benefit from a little more pattern and texture on the walls. Most designers advise against wallpaper (daily steam will most likely eventually cause it to peel or bubble), but it is possible to give bathroom walls a French wash, stencils, painted stripes, and other painted finishes. Stripes, either broad or combed on, can give texture and still look neat and tidy. Possibilities include pale cream with ivory, pale periwinkle blue and white, limestone beige or sand and off-white, or pale celadon and linen white.

Powder Room

Since this room is generally small and used infrequently, it's possible to use more dramatic, theatrical colors. Fresh choices include pale citron, lime, chartreuse, or cassis accents on white or ivory. These could be accented with gold leaf or silver leaf stripes along a molding, with interesting woods, or with quirky sculptural fittings in gold-tone brass or in nickel-plated brass. Still, it's generally more cost-effective and lasting to use classic materials and colors in a bathroom. Such timeless choices as pale pink/beige marble, buff wall paint, white and gray marble, neutral ivory and creamy colors, plus lots of white, look clean and fresh — and won't need to be replaced in a few years.

blue can give the naked body an unflattering cast. There's a reason why many designers today are using pink/beige and limestone and white — they are very flattering.

Cheerful

Sunny and pinkish tones of soft peach, palest cantaloupe, and pink grapefruit in all carefully controlled degrees of color saturation work exceptionally well as paint colors. Keep the color somewhat neutral — not fashion-y. If just a splash of color is needed, use it as a narrow border on floor tiles, or as an accent on the wall.

Brighten

To cheer up a dark, cool bathroom, consider pale golden (not acid) yellow with white trim. Avoid gray or dark blue. Brass fixtures — an elaborate faucet and handles — or an Edwardian-style bath set will brighten the room and work well with golden yellow paint.

ABOVE Creamy white is a timeless, classic bathroom color. Bathroom and chair design: Michael Berman, Los Angeles.

OPPOSITE Artful trim: A hand-stenciled border frames a gunnera leaf. Design: Waterman and Landenburger.

ABOVE Italian flavor: In a renovated house, with an understated Italian style, this bathroom is painted with colors tinted with umber, ocher, and sienna. Design: Thomas Bartlett, Napa Valley.

OPPOSITE Well balanced: When stone around the bath has pattern, simple finishes on the walls and shutters are often best. The arched mirror visually amplifies the room.

Year-round sunshine and Pacific Ocean currents keep spirits high in California. From Mendocino to Big Sur and San Francisco, from St. Helena to Santa Barbara, and from Los Angeles to all points north and south, decorators, architects, imaginative designers, impatient artists, and attentive store founders explore interior possibilities. Designers dream up plates and vases from raw clay, tables from raw metal, and hypnotic glass bowls and stone floors with little more than focus, skill, and optimism. For this updated listing, I have selected directional design stores, influential galleries and showrooms, plus salvage yards and quirky specialty stores. Most have originated from the passion and vision of one highly motivated founder and knowledgable owners. These stores and galleries capture the spirit and inspire return visits. Note a new listing of national catalogues for fine bed linens and bathroom essentials. *Diane Dorrans Saeks*

DESIGN & STYLE STORES

LOS ANGELES

Action Streets: Neighborhoods and recommended streets of fresh and intriguing style include North Robertson Avenue, Melrose Avenue (the western and eastern ends and highlights in between), Melrose Place (the real one), Beverly Boulevard, La Brea Avenue, Silver Lake, and out near the beach in Santa Monica. The fun is finding old stuff — gilt wood candlesticks, lighting, salvaged bathroom fixtures, garden antiques (to bring indoors), funky movie-set French furniture (which may have been sat on by Cary Grant or Fred Astaire), monogrammed sheets, vintage fabrics, steel hospital furniture, and patio chairs. Screeching to a halt in front of a chic store in a so-so part of town is bliss!

**AMERICAN RAG CIE
MAISON ET CAFE
148 S. La Brea Avenue
(Also in San Francisco)**
Cheerful handcrafted glasses, hand-painted plates, cozy custom upholstery. California/French style with Provençal pottery, books, and accessories for every room – plus a tiny cafe.

**ANICHINI
466 N. Robertson Boulevard**
Luxe. Bedroom glamour. Gorgeous silk-bound cashmere blankets, linen sheets, jacquard weave throws, and heirloom blankets.

**BRENDA ANTIN
7319 Beverly Boulevard**
Antique French and English garden decor outside catches the eye, but once inside this magical place, the senses are thrilled by English quilts, monogrammed white-linen slipcovers and lamp shades, French quilts, vintage French textiles, great, unusual colors everywhere.

**BLACKMAN-CRUZ
800 N. La Cienega Boulevard**
Highly individual, desirable stuff, so you have to keep coming back. Sculptural and often rather odd and wonderful twentieth-century objects and furniture. Architectural fragments. A favorite with architects and Hollywood set designers.

**BOOK SOUP
8818 Sunset Boulevard
West Hollywood**
Must-visit bookstore, with all-day and midnight browsing. Superb selections of design, architecture, and photography books. Open-air magazine stand has every international design magazine. Bistro.

**CITY ANTIQUES
8444 Melrose Avenue**
A great source for eighteenth-through twentieth-century furniture, some by admired but slightly obscure designers. An eclectic, influential look.

**NANCY CORZINE
8747 Melrose Avenue**
To the trade only. Elegant, suave, sexy updated classic furnishings. Outstanding Italian fabric collection.

**DIALOGICA
8304 Melrose Avenue**
Smooth contemporary/thirties-influenced furniture.

**DIAMOND FOAM & FABRIC
611 S. La Brea Avenue**
Success! Jason Asch's empire expands along La Brea. Style insiders' favorite for instant fabric gratifications, excellent prices. Now a not-so-secret trade source for basic and decorative this-minute fabrics. Easy to find here are simple and luxurious textiles – velvets, linen, chintz, silk, damask, twills, challis, terry, all in just the right colors. (Pop in to La Brea Bakery, opposite, for superb anise and fig bread loaves.)

DIVA

**Corner of Beverly Boulevard
and N. Robertson Drive**

In the heart of the to-the-trade design center. Offers all the contemporary design icons – like Philippe Starck – that could be on every corner in Los Angeles and are rare. (Designers in Southern California prefer the past.)

RANDY FRANKS

8448 Melrose Place

One-of-a-kind furniture. New designers.

HOLLYHOCK

214 N. Larchmont Boulevard

A cheerful, elegant look. Furniture, mirrors, and decorative accessories for rooms and gardens.

INDIGO SEAS

123 N. Robertson Boulevard

Gin Fizz anyone? Lynn von Kersting's style: part Caribbean Colonial outpost, part Riviera, part romanticized England. Witty. Sofas, silver, soaps.

LIEF

8922 Beverly Boulevard

Elegant pared-down Gustavian antiques and simple Scandinavian Biedermeier are a refreshing change from Fine French Furniture.

LIZ'S ANTIQUE HARDWARE

453 S. La Brea

Hardware for doors, windows, and bathrooms, plus lighting from 1850 to 1950. Styles include Spanish, Victorian, Arts & Crafts, art deco.

LA MAISON DU BAL

705 N. Harper Avenue

Antique and vintage textiles, furniture, lighting.

MODERNICA

7366 Beverly Boulevard

Modernist furniture, focusing on twenties to sixties.

**RICHARD MULLIGAN-SUNSET
COTTAGE**

8157 Sunset Boulevard

To the trade only: 213-650-8660. Great style. Entrancing mise en scene. With your decorator in tow, get seduced by Mulligan's completely chic and sophisticated country vision. Richard and Mollie have star power – and a devoted following among old-timers, Hollywood designers, and celebs. Antique and vintage country-style antiques. Finely finessed painted reproductions and collectible paintings, pottery, one-of-a-kind lamps.

ODALISQUE

7278 Beverly Boulevard

Linger among the funky antiques, vintage silks, chandeliers, and pillows. Surprising and quirky. Antique fabrics. One-of-a-kind pillows and draperies made from embroidered ecclesiastical fabrics.

PACIFIC DESIGN CENTER

8687 Melrose Avenue

To-the-trade showrooms such as Mimi London, Donghia, Randolph & Hein, Snaidero, McGuire, Brunschwig & Fils, Baker, Oakmont, and Kneedler-Fauchere present the finest fabrics, furniture, lighting, rugs, hardware, reproductions, decorative accessories, fixtures. Very professional, totally top-of-the-line.

RIZZOLI BOOKSTORE

**9501 Wilshire Boulevard
(Also in Santa Monica)**

Outstanding selection of design and architecture books. Browse among the elegantly arranged stacks. Open late.

ROOMS

619 N. Croft Avenue

By appointment: 213-655-9813. Interior designer Michael Berman's studio with his custom-made furniture.

**ROSE TARLOW–
MELROSE HOUSE**

8454 Melrose Place

Rose Tarlow, designer and lecturer, has a fine-tuned sense of scale, along with a dash of humor. Her furniture collection demonstrates an understanding of comfort, elegance, line, and grace. A certain Continental/English sensibility, languor, and timeless glamour.

RUSSELL SIMPSON COMPANY

8109 Melrose Avenue

Bret Witke and Diane Rosenstein sell furniture from the forties and fifties. Eames, Jacobsen, Saarinen, Robsjohn-Gibbings, et al.

VIRTUE

149 S. La Brea Avenue

Andrew Virtue's fresh and totally chic antiques and decoration shop. Madeleine Castaing and Elsie de Wolfe live on! Colorful, witty, and joyful. Garden furniture you can bring indoors, paintings, pillows.

**W ANTIQUES AND
ECCENTRICITIES**

8925 Melrose Avenue

Melissa Wallace Deitz's domain – an effervescent gallery selling everything from eighteenth-century gilded chairs to birdcage-shaped chandeliers, fountains, urns, art deco furniture. It's one of a kind and ever changing.

My definitive list of the best design and style stores includes all my favorite shopping streets: Fillmore, Hayes, Brady (off Market), Post, Sutter, Sacramento, Gough, Geary, Union Square and Street, the northern end of Polk. For top-notch stores, explore Fillmore Street — from Pacific Avenue to Bush Street. Then march along Sacramento Street. And don't forget South Park, South of Market, and the Mission District.

AD/50
711 Sansome Street
New downtown location for modernist and contemporary furniture (including designs by Park Furniture and Christopher Deam).

AGRARIA
1051 Howard Street
A fragrant favorite. Maurice Gibson and Stanford Stevenson's classic candles, potpourri, and soaps are tops. (Best selection is at Gump's.)

ARCH
407 Jackson Street
Architect Susan Colliver's colorful shop sells supplies for designers, architects, and artists — and home improvement fanatics. Excellent range of papers.

BANANA REPUBLIC
256 Grant Avenue
Sparkling new flagship store includes a refined home department. Well-priced dinnerware, crystal, frames, silk pillows, linens.

THE BATH & BEYOND
135 Mississippi Street
Bath and kitchen showroom displays a tantalizing selection of baths, whirlpools, fittings and fixtures.

BELL'OCCHIO
8 Brady Street
Claudia Schwartz and Toby Hanson's whimsical boutique offers soaps, hand-painted ribbons, French silk flowers. Trips to Paris produce charming antiques, hats, posters, and retro-chic Parisian face powders.

GORDON BENNETT
2102 Union Street
Fresh garden style throughout the seasons. Vases, plants, books, candles, decoupage plates, and tools. Ask the owner to explain the name — and to introduce his standard poodles.

BLOOMERS
2975 Washington Street
Top people speed-dial Patric Powell's fragrant domain. Bloomers offers the freshest cut flowers (totally tasteful) and unusual orchids in terra cotta pots. Dozens of vases, French ribbons, and baskets. Nothing overdone or tricked-up here — just nature's natural beauty.

VIRGINIA BREIER
3091 Sacramento Street
A gallery for contemporary and traditional American crafts.

BRITEX
146 Geary Street
Excellent for home sewers. Growing home design sections. Action central for thousands of fabrics. World-class selections of classic and unusual furnishing textiles, braids, notions.

BROWN DIRT COWBOYS
2418 Polk Street
Painted and refurbished furniture, housewares.

BULGARI
237 Post Street
Browse in the superb upstairs silver department — it's heaven — then bestow something sparkling and elegant upon yourself.

CANDELIER
60 Maiden Lane
Wade Benson's beautifully styled candles, books, vases, and home accoutrements. Candlesticks and tabletop decor.

THOMAS E. CARA
517 Pacific Avenue
Espresso machines and hardware — a long-time company, very authoritative.

CARTIER
231 Post Street
Elegant selection of accessories, silver, crystal, vases, porcelain.

CLERVI MARBLE COMPANY
221 Bayshore Boulevard
This esteemed 80-year-old company sells a handsome collection of limestone, travertine, onyx, marble, granite, and slate. Every stone is fabricated to order.

COLUMBINE DESIGN
1541 Grant Avenue
In North Beach, Kathleen Dooley displays fresh flowers, gifts, along with shells, graphic framed butterflies, bugs, and beetles.

CS BATH
566 Minnesota Street
(Also in San Leandro)
This showroom displays top fittings and fixtures for bath and kitchen. Extensive display of hardware.

THE COTTAGE TABLE COMPANY
550 18th Street.
Tony Cowan's heirloom-quality hardwood tables to order. Shipping available.

DE VERA
580 Sutter Street
Magic shop. A must-visit, one-of-a-kind store. *Objets trouvés,* sculpture, Venetian glass, original small-scale finds, and original designs by Federico de Vera. De Vera recently opened a new jewel-box store at 29 Maiden Lane, selling small, precious objets d'art.

DE VERA GLASS
384 Hayes Street
A vibrant gallery of singular glass objects by contemporary American artists, along with Venetian and Scandinavian classics. Unusual colors.

DANDELION/TAMPOPO
55 Potrero Avenue
Old favorite. Japanese-influenced aesthetic, antiques — very versatile.

DECORUM
1400 Vallejo Street
Jack Beeler's art deco domain. Superb lighting, furniture. Open Saturdays.

EARTHSAKE
2076 Chestnut Street
(Also in the Embarcadero Center in San Francisco, and in Berkeley and Palo Alto)
Earth-friendly stores with pure and simple furniture, untreated bed linens and towels, vases of recycled glass, candles.

F. DORIAN
388 Hayes Street
Treasures galore — at excellent prices. Contemporary accessories, folk arts, and antiques.

FILLAMENTO
2185 Fillmore Street
Trend alert! For more than a dozen years, a museum for design aficionados. Owner Iris Fuller stacks three floors with style-conscious furniture, tableware, towels, mirrors, glass, toiletries, and gifts. Iris is first with new designers and supports local talent, including Nik Weinstein, Willsea O'Brien, Ann Gish, Annieglass, and Cyclamen. Frames, lamps, linens, beds, and partyware.

FIORIDELLA
1920 Polk Street
For more than 17 years, this store has been offering the most beautiful flowers and plants. Fine selection of decorative accessories and versatile vases.

FLAX ART AND DESIGN
1699 Market Street
Tempting, exhaustive selections of frames, paper, lighting, tabletop accessories, boxes, art books, furnishings. One-stop shopping for art supplies. Catalogue.

FORZA
1742 Polk Street
Handcrafted furniture, candles, accessories with an urbane elegance. Great aesthetic.

GALLERIA DESIGN CENTER, THE SAN FRANCISCO DESIGN CENTER AND SHOWPLACE DESIGN CENTER
Henry Adams Street
Come to this South of Market design center with your decorator or architect. Selections and temptations are extraordinary. A professional's eye can lead you to the right chairs, tables, sofas, trims, silks, accessories, fabrics. These to-the-trade-only buildings — along with Showplace West and other nearby showrooms — offer top-of-the-line furniture, fabrics, and furnishings. Randolph & Hein, Kneedler-Fauchere, Sloan Miyasato, Shears & Window, Clarence House, Jack Lenor Larsen, Palacek, Brunschwig & Fils, Kallista, DJ Mehler, Schumacher, Therien Studio, McRae Hinckley, Donghia, Summit Furniture, Enid Ford, and Houles are personal favorites. (Purchases may also be made through a buying service.) Explore the neighborhood and find Waterworks, Therien & Co (Scandinavian, Continental, and English antiques), Robert Hering antiques, and the handsome, almost-residential Palladian outpost of Ed Hardy San Francisco (eclectic antiques, garden antiques, and worldly reproductions).

STANLEE R. GATTI FLOWERS
Fairmont Hotel, Nob Hill
Fresh flowers, Agraria potpourri, vases, and candles.

GEORGE
2411 California Street
Style for dogs and cats, including dog beds, Todd Oldham- and Tom Bonauro-designed charms, toys, cedar pillows, bowls and accessories. Best dog treats: handmade whole-grain biscuits.

GREEN WORLD MERCANTILE
2340 Polk Street
Earth-friendly housewares, clothing, gardening equipment, books, and unpretentious decorative accessories. Plants and gardening equipment.

GUMP'S
135 Post Street
Visionary Geraldine Stutz and her snappy team dreamed up this new, chic Gump's — with superbly selected fine crafts, art, Orient-inspired accessories, plus tip-top names in silver, crystal. Cushy and very elegant bed linens. An essential stop. Be sure to visit the Treillage garden antiques shop, and the decorative glass departments. Catalogue.

GYPSY HONEYMOON
Corner of 24th Street and
Guerrero streets
Magical and romantic decor.
Art glass, refurbished furniture,
beds, old mirrors, trunks, framed
vintage prints.

HERMES
212 Stockton Street
Silk scarves here are the ulti-
mate, but climb the limestone
stairs to find tableware, blankets, towels, cashmere throws,
picnicware, silver, chic decor.

RICHARD HILKERT BOOKS
333 Hayes Street
Like a gentleman's library.
Designers and book addicts
telephone Richard to order
out-of-print style books and
newest design books. Browse
here, buy, then stroll to the
Opera or the Symphony.

IN MY DREAMS
1300 Pacific Avenue
Jewelry designer Harry Fireside's
dreamy shop for soaps, antiques,
and Chinese lanterns.

JAPONESQUE
824 Montgomery Street
Passionate Koichi Hara demonstrates his lifelong devotion to
refinement, tradition, harmony,
simplicity, and natural materials.
Japanese sculpture, glass, furniture. Timeless and tranquil
gallery.

FORREST JONES
3274 Sacramento Street
A Pacific Heights favorite.
Baskets, housewares, porcelain,
excellent lamps.

JUICY NEWS
2453 Fillmore Street
A jumping joint for every
possible international fashion,
design, architecture, and style
magazine – and fresh fruit
refreshments.

KRIS KELLY
One Union Square
Selections of beds, fine linens,
and table linens.

SUE FISHER KING
3067 Sacramento Street
Sleeping beauties for bed-lovers.
Sue King's Italian, French, and
English bed linens, cashmere
throws, and tableware are the
chic-est and prettiest. Luxurious
blankets, hand-dyed Himalayan
cashmere fringed throws, silk
pillows, plus accessories, books,
soaps, furniture, and Diptyque
candles.

LIMN
290 Townsend Street
The place to be on Saturday
afternoons – after the Farmers'
Market at Ferry Plaza. One of
only a handful of Northern California stores selling top-of-the-
line contemporary furniture,
accessories, and lighting by more
than 300 international manufacturers. Well-priced, to-go
collections along with to-order
Philippe Starck, B & B Italia,
Andree Putman, and Mathieu
& Ray, plus top Northern California talent. Ceramics by
Cyclamen. Visit the new gallery
behind the store.

DAVID LUKE & ASSOCIATE
773 14th Street
Antiques, vintage tableware,
funky furniture, old garden ornaments – some of it from the
estates of England. (David's
boxer, Baby, is his associate.)

MAC
1543 Grant Avenue
Chris Ospital's trend-setting
salon sells style inspiration and
accessories. Stop and chat:
talent-spotter Chris knows
who's new.

MACY'S
Union Square
Extensive bed linens department
– excellent selection of down
comforters. Furniture and accessories floors and the Interior
Design Department are now in
the old Emporium building on
Market Street.

MAISON D'ETRE
92 South Park
In a Toby Levy-designed building,
changing collections of vintage
garden furniture (for indoors),
lighting, hand-blown glass bowls
by local artists, candlesticks,
metal vases, candles. Presented
with spirit.

DJ MEHLER COLLECTIONS
Showplace Design Center
San Francisco Design Center
2 Henry Adams Street
Outstanding collections from
top American and European fit-
tings and fixtures manufacturers.
Excellent service.

MIKE FURNITURE
Corner of Fillmore and
Sacramento streets
Directed by Mike Moore and
partner Mike Thakar and their
energetic crew, this friendly,
sunny store offers updated furniture classics-with-a-twist by
Mike Studio, Beverly, and other
manufacturers. Custom and
bespoke design here is very
accessible. One-stop shopping
for fast-delivery sofas, blankets,
fabrics, lamps, tables, fabrics,
accessories.

NAOMI'S ANTIQUES TO GO
1817 Polk Street
American art pottery! Bauer
and Fiesta, of course, plus historic studio pottery. American
railroad, hotel, luxury liner,
Navy, dude ranch, and bus
depot china.

NEST
2300 Fillmore Street

In a sunny Victorian building where a friendly pharmacy operated for decades, Marcella Madsen and Judith Gilman have feathered their enchanting Nest. Seductive treasure trove includes books, silk flowers, antique beds, Shabby Chic sheets, rustic French antiques, Italian prints, sachets, sofa, and Bravura lamp shades and pillows.

PAINT EFFECTS
2426 Fillmore Street

Paint a bed! Colorful! Inspiring. Sheila Rauch and partner Patricia Orlando have a fanatical following for their innovative paints and tools. Hands-on paint technique classes by talented Lesley Ruda, along with everything for French washes, gilding, liming, crackle glazing, decoupage, stenciling, and other fine finishes.

PAXTON GATE
1204 Stevenson Street

Peter Kline and Sean Quigley's gardening store offers uncommon plants (such as sweetly scented Buddha's Hand citron trees), vases, and hand-forged tools.

POLANCO
393 Hayes Street

Superbly presented Mexican fine arts, photography, and crafts. Museum curator Elsa Cameron says you can't find better quality anywhere in Mexico.

POLO RALPH LAUREN
Crocker Galleria, corner of Post and Kearney streets

Ralph Lauren's handsome emporium purveys the complete Home collection. Great beds. Best-quality furniture, accessories, beds, towels, linens, and the trappings of fine rooms, country houses.

POTTERY BARN
Stores throughout California

This on-a-roll San Francisco-based company has stores all over the country, including New York. New full-service design stores offer furniture, rugs, beds, sheets, draperies, special orders. Practical, well-priced home style. Excellent bedroom basics. Classic, accessible design. Outstanding catalogue.

RAYON VERT
3187 16th Street

Brilliant floral designer Kelly Kornegay's garden of earthly delights just got bigger – and better. Vintage furniture, Oriental porcelains, flowers, artifacts, glasses, architectural fragments in a full-tilt, humble-chic setting.

RH
2506 Sacramento Street

Sunny garden and tableware store has beeswax candles, vases, goblets. Inspiring selection of cachepots, vases. Topiaries, too.

RIZZOLI BOOKS
117 Post Street

Library-like, well-located near the Gap, Polo, Diesel, TSE, Gump's. Book-lovers' paradise. Outstanding collection of design, architecture, and photography books. Cafe.

SAN FRANCISCO MUSEUM OF MODERN ART
151 Third Street

Outstanding design and art books, modernist accessories, framed posters, handcrafted designs by local artists.

SATIN MOON FABRICS
32 Clement Street

Twenty-six-year-old store sells a well-edited collection of decorating linens, trims, chintzes, and other well-priced fabrics.

SCHEUER LINENS
340 Sutter Street

Fine-quality bed linens, towels, blankets. The staff facilitates custom orders particularly well.

SHABBY CHIC
3075 Sacramento Street
(Also in Los Angeles)

A local favorite. Specializes in fat and slimmed-down chairs and cozy sofas with comfortable airs and loose-fitting slipcovers.

SLIPS
1534 Grant Avenue

Sami Rosenzweig's spirit lives on! Custom-made slipcovers for chairs, headboards, and sofas, plus draperies, ottomans.

SUE FISHER KING HOME AT WILKES BASHFORD
375 Sutter Street

Luscious luxuries. Sue's obsessive perfectionism is evident in her selections of Ann Gish linens, Venetian and Florentine cashmere throws, beds, hand-blown glass, Venetian pillows, and special *objets d'art* from Italy, France, London. Books.

TIFFANY & CO
350 Post Street

Lust for a sapphire ring, or a Paloma Picasso necklace, then step upstairs to the venerated crystal, china, and silver departments. Order Elsa Peretti's classic glasses, bowls, and silver.

WILLIAMS-SONOMA
150 Post Street
(and around the country)
Everything for cooks and kitchens – or breakfast in bed. Flagship for the Williams-Sonoma cookware empire. Stores throughout the state, including Corte Madera, Palo Alto, Pasadena. Delicacies. Quality, lifetime basics for both serious and dilettante cooks. Excellent catalogues.

ANN SACKS TILE AND STONE
Showplace Design Center
2 Henry Adams Street
Extensive selection of hand-crafted tiles, plus stone cut in many sizes. Some historical designs.

WATERWORKS
235 Kansas Street
The pre-eminent source for limited-production tile and bath fixtures and fittings. Waterworks products, made in small factories and artisans' studios, echo the quality of the past.

WILLIAM STOUT ARCHITECTURAL BOOKS
804 Montgomery Street
The best! Architect Bill Stout's chock-a-block book store specializes in basic and wonderfully obscure twentieth-century architecture publications, along with new and out-of-print interior design and garden books. Catalogues.

WORLDWARE
336 Hayes Street
Friendly chic style and design. Shari Sant's eco-store sells cozy sheets and blankets, and such delights as patchwork pillows, aromatherapy candles. Interiors crafted by Dan Plummer from salvaged materials.

ZINC DETAILS
1905 Fillmore Street
The vibrant store has a cult following. Well-priced contemporary furniture, lighting. Hand-blown glass vases and lamp shades by California artists. Domain of Wendy Nishimura and Vasilios Kiniris. (No, they don't sell anything made of zinc.)

ZONAL HOME INTERIORS
568 Hayes Street
Russell Pritchard's pioneering store presents rustic furniture and decorative objects. He made rust and the friendly textures of loving use fashionable. Old Americana at its most whimsical.

BERKELEY, ELMWOOD

Head over the Bay Bridge. Design store action here is focused on wonderfully revived Fourth Street. We recommend, too, a detour to Cafe Fanny, the Acme Bread bakery, Chez Panisse, and the Elmwood neighborhood.

BERKELEY MILLS
2830 Seventh Street
Handcrafted Japanese- and Mission-influenced furniture. Blends the best of old-world craftsmanship and high-tech methods. Catalogue.

BUILDERS BOOKSOURCE
1817 Fourth Street
(Also in San Francisco)
Well-considered design, architecture, gardening, and building books.

CAMPS AND COTTAGES
2109 Virginia Street
Visit the cafe at Chez Panisse or the great Cheese Board, then pop in for a visit. Charming homey furniture and low-key accessories. Adirondack styles.

ELICA'S PAPERS
1801 Fourth Street
Japanese handmade papers. Custom-made stationery, albums, frames, paper wall-hangings, decorative boxes, sketchbooks, some from mulberry bark. Papers can be used for making lamp shades, window shades, screens, even wallpaper.

THE GARDENER
1836 Fourth Street
Pioneer Alta Tingle's brilliant, bustling garden-style store sells vases, books, tables, chairs, paintings, clothing, toiletries, and tools for nature-lovers – whether they have a garden or are just dreaming. Asian antiques, terra cotta pots. Consistently original, classic style.

LIGHTING STUDIO
1808 Fourth Street
Lighting design services. Cheery and chic contemporary lamps.

THE MAGAZINE
1823 Eastshore Highway
Four-year-old store sells contemporary American and European designs. Artemide, Flos, Flexform, Aero, and Cappellini, and many others.

OMEGA TOO
2204 San Pablo Avenue
Gold – from salvaged houses in the area. Building materials, fixtures, lighting, plus treasures. Some aficionados mine this store and sibling Ohmega Salvage at 2407 San Pablo Avenue weekly.

RESTORATION HARDWARE
1733 Fourth Street
Great resources for fixtures – including antique-style hardware and fittings. Excellent lighting, quirky accessories, draperies, bathroom hardware, tools, books, candles. Founded in California, the company now has more than 30 stores around the country.

SUR LA TABLE
1806 Fourth Street
Outpost of the 24-year-old Seattle cookware company but feels entirely original to Berkeley. In a 5,000-square-foot "warehouse," the shop stocks every goodie, gadget, tool, utensil, plate, machine, and kitchen decoration for serious and dilettante cooks. Catalogue, too.

TAIL OF THE YAK
2632 Ashby Avenue
Longtime partners Alice Hoffman Erb and Lauren Adams Allard have created a magical mystery store that is always worth a trip – across the Bay or across the Atlantic. Whimsical vases, accessories, wedding gifts, Mexican furniture, fabrics, ribbons, notecards, Lauren's books, linens, and antique jewelry.

ERICA TANOV
3032 Claremont Avenue
The place for linen pajamas, romantic bed accessories. Erica's lace-edged sheets and shams, and linen duvet covers are quietly luxurious. (Drop into Oliveto Restaurant, the Rockridge Market Hall, Maison d'Etre, and Grace Bakery just up the street.)

URBAN ORE
1333 Sixth Street
One city block of salvaged architecture and house throw-aways. Doors, windowframes, shutters, lighting fixtures, furniture, and vintage fixtures. An adventure!

ZIA HOUSEWORKS
1310 Tenth Street
Colin Smith's sun-filled gallery-store offers a vivid variety of hand-crafted furniture designs and art. Mike Furniture Studio and Maine Cottage collections.

BIG SUR

THE PHOENIX
Highway 1
An enduring store where you can linger for hours to the sound of wind chimes. Handcrafted decorative objects, candles, glass, books, sculpture, woven throws, hand-knit sweaters by Kaffe Fassett (who grew up in Big Sur), and soaps. Coast views from all windows. Be sure to walk downstairs. Crystals and handmade objects on all sides. Visit Nepenthe restaurant up the hill. The sixties spirit lives on in Big Sur. Still gorgeous after all these years.

CARMEL

CARMEL BAY COMPANY
Corner of Ocean and Lincoln
Tableware, books, glassware, furniture, prints.

FRANCESCA VICTORIA
250 Crossroads Boulevard
Decorative accessories for garden and home. Fresh style.

LUCIANO ANTIQUES
San Carlos and Fifth streets
Cosmopolitan antiques. Wander through the vast rooms – to view furniture, lighting, sculpture, and handsome reproductions.

PLACES IN THE SUN
Dolores Avenue, near Ocean Avenue
Decor from sunny climes. Provençal tables, Mexican candlesticks, colorful fabrics.

CARMEL VALLEY

TANCREDI & MORGEN
Valley Hills Shopping Center
Carmel Valley Road
Chic, understated country style. Bed dressing, vintage vases, fabrics, chairs, rustic ornament.

CORTE MADERA

RESTORATION HARDWARE
1700 Redwood Highway
Handsome, airy store offering finishing touches for interiors and exteriors. Hardware, lighting, furniture, accessories, weather vanes, books, kitchen gadgets, gardening tools.

FORT BRAGG

STUDIO Z MENDOCINO
711 North Main Street
Interior designers like Michael Berman and Barbara Barry love Zida Borcich – one of the last letterpress printers. She handsets old letterpress ornaments on fine papers and prints on antique presses. Her goldfoil and black logos – flowers, teapots, bees, dragonflies, a chef, a watering can – are chic and smart for modern correspondence and letter writing in bed. (Phone 707-964-2522 for an appointment.)

GLEN ELLEN

THE OLIVE PRESS
Jack London Village
14301 Arnold Drive
Everything pertaining to olives – including hand-blown martini glasses. Extra-virgin olive oils, cooking equipment, tableware, toiletries, linens.

HEALDSBURG

JIMTOWN STORE
6706 State Highway 128
Cycle on country roads to J. Carrie Brown and John Werner's friendly store in the Alexander Valley. The Mercantile & Exchange vintage Americana is cheerful and very well-priced.

SOTOYOME TOBACCO COMPANY
119 Plaza Street
Myra and Wade Hoefer's chic cigar store in a Greek Revival building – originally a Bank of America. The name is that of the original Spanish land grant upon which Healdsburg was founded. Humidors, French silver cutters, cigar posters, and cigars.

MENLO PARK

MILLSTREET
1131 Chestnut Street
Objects of desire: Continental antiques, Ann Gish bed linens and silks, Tuscan pottery, tapestries, orchids, mirrors, botanical prints, silk and cashmere throws.

MENDOCINO

When in Mendocino, be sure to make a dinner reservation at Cafe Beaujolais.

FITTINGS FOR HOME AND GARDEN
45050 Main Street
Furniture, lighting, hardware, accessories. Large selection of garden tools and lamps.

THE GOLDEN GOOSE
45094 Main Street
An enduring favorite. Superb, pristine classic linens, antiques, overlooking the Headlands and the ocean. Baby linens, cashmere and merino throws. The most stylish store in Mendocino.

LARK IN THE MORNING
10460 Kasten Street
Handcrafted musical instruments to display and play. Traditional harps, guitars, violins, as well as ethnic instruments from around the world: ouds, bagpipes, pennywhistles, flutes – and CDs.

STICKS
45085 Albion Street
The utterly charming "twigs and branches" store of Bob Keller. Rustic furniture, decor, and accessories – without the cliches. Great chairs, willow headboards.

WILKESSPORT
10466 Lansing Street
In addition to nifty sportswear, Wilkes Bashford offers David Luke antiques, crafts of the region, and paintings.

MILL VALLEY

CAPRICORN ANTIQUES & COOKWARE
100 Throckmorton Avenue
This quiet, reliable store seems to have been here forever. Basic cookware, along with antique tables, dressers, and cupboards.

PRAIRIE GARDEN
14 Miller Avenue
Garden style for indoors or out. Furniture, plants, great color palette.

PULLMAN & CO
108 Throckmorton Street
Luxurious bed linens, along with furniture, lamps, tableware, and accessories.

SMITH & HAWKEN
35 Corte Madera
The original. Nursery (begun under horticulturist Sarah Hammond's superb direction) and store. Everything for gardens. Also in Pacific Heights, Berkeley, Palo Alto, Los Gatos, Santa Rosa, and points beyond. Catalogue.

SUMMER HOUSE GALLERY
21 Throckmorton Street
Impossible to leave empty-handed. Artist-crafted accessories and (to order) comfortable sofas and chairs. Witty hand-crafted frames, glassware, candlesticks, and colorful accessories. Slipcovered loveseats, vases, tables, gifts.

MONTECITO

BILL CORNFIELD GALLERY
539 San Ysidro Road
Indian, European, European antiques. Very eclectic, charming.

PIERRE LAFOND/ WENDY FOSTER
516 San Ysidro Road
Handsomely displayed household furnishings, books, accessories, and South American and Malabar Coast furniture. Beautiful linens.

WILLIAM LAMAN
1496 E. Valley Road
Country antiques, casual furniture, garden accessories.

OAKLAND

MAISON D'ETRE
5330 College Avenue
Indoor/outdoor style. Eccentric, and whimsical decorative objects and furniture for rooms and gardens.

OAKVILLE

OAKVILLE GROCERY
7856 St. Helena Highway
No visit to the Napa Valley would be complete without a stop here. Extraordinary wine selection, prepared foods, local olive oils, herbs, international cheeses, organic coffees, and locally baked artisan breads. Everything for breakfast in bed, picnics, parties. (Check out Dean & DeLuca in St. Helena, too.)

PALO ALTO

BELL'S BOOKS
536 Emerson Street
Reading-in-bed lovers alert! Walls of fine and scholarly selections of new, vintage, and rare books on every aspect of interior design, gardens, and gardening. Also literature, books on decorative arts, photography, cooking.

HILLARY THATZ
Stanford Shopping Center
Thorough. A dreamy view of the interiors of England, as seen by Cheryl Driver. Traditional accessories, furniture, frames, and decorative objects. Garden furnishings.

POLO-RALPH LAUREN
Stanford Shopping Center
Definitive. Just gets better and better – great versatile decor, linens, blankets. A spacious, gracious store. The expanding world imagined through Ralph Lauren's eyes. Outstanding

selection of furniture, imaginary heritage accessories. Catalogue.

PASADENA

HORTUS
284 E. Orange Grove Boulevard
Superbly selected perennials, antique roses, and a full nursery. Handsome collection of antique garden ornaments.

SAN ANSELMO

MODERN i 1950
500 Red Hill Avenue

Steven Cabella is passionate about modernism and time-warp mid-century (1935-65) furnishings. Vintage furnishings, Eames chairs, furniture by architects, objects, and artwork. Located in a restored modernist architect's office building.

SAN RAFAEL

MANDERLEY
By appointment: 415-472-6166.
Ronnie Wells' one-of-a-kind silk shams, antique fabrics, and vintage pillows set trends.

ST. HELENA

BALE MILL DESIGN
3431 North St. Helena Highway
Decorative and practical up-dated classic furniture in a wide range of styles. A favorite with decorators. Ira Yaeger paintings.

CALLA LILY
1222 Main Street
Elegant European luxury bed linens, accessories, frames.

SHOWPLACE NORTH
1350 Main Street
(Also in Santa Rosa and Carmel)
Interior design, fabrics, custom furniture.

ST. HELENA ST. HELENA ANTIQUES
1231 Main Street
(Yes, the name is intentionally repetitious.) Rustic furniture, vintage wine paraphernalia, vintage accessories.

TANTAU
1220 Adams Street
Charming atmosphere. Decorative accessories, furniture, hand-painted furniture, gifts.

TESORO
649 Main Street
Fresh-flower heaven. Topiaries, wreaths – vases, too.

TIVOLI
1432 Main Street
Tom Scheibal and partners have created a sunny indoor/outdoor garden furniture and accessories store. Tables and chairs and occasional pieces in iron, aluminum, concrete, and recycled redwood. Antique garden ornaments.

VANDERBILT & CO
1429 Main Street
(Also at the Stanford Shopping Center)
Extensive collections of luxury bed linens, books, glassware, hand-painted Italian ceramics, accessories. A year-round favorite in the wine country.

SANTA MONICA

THOMAS CALLAWAY BENCHWORKS, INC.
2929 Nebraska Avenue
By appointment: 310-828-9379.
Interior designer/actor Thomas Callaway designs, makes and offers custom-made star-quality arm chairs, sofas, and ottomans with deep-down comfort and timeless glamour. These are future heirlooms, very collectible.

HENNESSY & INGALLS
1254 Third Street, Promenade
Architects and designers flock to this book store, which specializes in the widest range of architectural books.

KATHRYN IRELAND
1118 Montana Avenue
Kathryn's eclectic and versatile new fabrics and furnishings are inspired by timeless English, French, and ethnic motifs.

JASPER
1454 Fifth Street
Interior designer Michael Smith's brilliant store and atelier. In a cool, sleek former art gallery, this high-ceilinged studio displays bold vignettes of chairs, antiques from around the world, linens, cashmeres, art glass, and Smith's own designs. Worth a detour from anywhere.

LIEF MONTANA
1010 Montana Avenue
Clean-lined Scandinavian antiques with a light touch. Gustavian-style bedroom furniture.

ROOM WITH A VIEW
1600 Montana Avenue
Children's furnishings, and especially glamorous bed linens by the likes of Cocoon (silks), Bischoff, and Anichini.

SHABBY CHIC
1013 Montana Avenue
Yes, they still do great smooshy sofas, but they've also moved on to tailored upholstery and a new line of fabrics.

SANTA ROSA

RANDOLPH JOHNSON STUDIO
608 Fifth Street
Master craftsman/designer Randy Johnson makes dreamy furniture and accessories with superb detail in a wide range of styles. Draperies, painted finishes. Finest custom artistry.

SONOMA

SLOAN AND JONES
First Street West,
on the square.
Ann Jones and Sheelagh Sloan run and stock this splendid antiques store. Set in a fine old corner building, it's the place for country porcelains, silverware, Asian vintage furniture, photography, linens, and table accessories.

STUDIO SONOMA
380 First Street West
Designer Robin Nelson offers beautifully edited home furnishings, paintings, slipcovers, lighting. Seasonal delights – including hammocks for summer, quilts for winter.

VENICE

BOUNTIFUL
1335 Abbott Kinney Boulevard
By appointment: 310-450-3620.
Vintage Edwardian and Victorian painted furniture, lamps, old beds, quirky *objets.* This is a street and a neighborhood to explore.

FLEA MARKETS

Flea-market fans in Los Angeles head for Long Beach or Pasadena fleas, and catch up with San Francisco's roving band. Old, small towns in California's hinterlands often surprise with inexpensive, quirky antiques. In dusty, cob-webbed shops you may find heirloom linens and laces, old brass beds, Victorian chairs, Lalique vases, botanical prints, and hand-bound books, rusty tools, tins, and old signs. These are the eccentricities that give rooms texture and individuality. As any serious style watcher will tell you, watch for newspaper listings of auctions, antiques sales, estate sales, weekend flea markets, and seasonal vintage and antique furniture shows.

MAIL-ORDER

The following national specialty catalogues offer the best mail-order bedroom and bathroom accoutrements – beds (basic and beautiful), luxurious and basic linens, mattresses, duvets, bedroom carpets, and custom-made pillows and bedcovers. From these outstanding catalogues, it would be tempting to outfit a palace – or a cozy cabin in the woods. Most catalogues include a selection of baby's and children's bed linens and bedroom furniture. One bed linens and towels extra to recommend: free monogramming.

BERGDORF GOODMAN
P.O. BOX 660598
Dallas, TX 75266
800-964-8619
Pampering – with silken duvets fluffed with silk floss, silk and Merino wool blankets, Frette's best sheets, and heirloom trousseau linens. Very luxurious.

BLOOMINGDALE'S
(Stores around the country)
800-967-3788
Seasonal catalogues sell a broad swathe of housewares – from fine basic linens and pillows to substantial furniture.

E. BRAUN
717 Madison Avenue
New York, NY
212-838-6793
These are the fine traditional bed linens of the Upper East Side in Manhattan that brides dream of for their boudoirs. Lace-trimmed sheets, exquisitely detailed silk bedcovers, beautiful hand-embroidered pillowcases.

CALICO CORNERS
203 Gale Lane
Kennett Square, PA 19348
800-213-6366
Ralph Lauren classic fabrics, along with ready-made bedding and accessories.

CHAMBERS
P.O. Box 7841
San Francisco, CA 94120
800-334-9790
Superb seasonal selections of fine European- and American-made bed linens, alpaca and silk blankets, outstanding towels (to be monogrammed), cashmere bedcovers, bedroom furniture, bathroom accessories, floor coverings, and toiletries.

COMING HOME
1 Lands' End Lane
Dodgeville, WI 53595
800-345-3696
Well-priced bed basics, plus lots of goosedown comforters in a range of styles. Natural cotton sheets, blankets, towels.

THE COMPANY STORE
500 Company Store Road
La Crosse WI 54601
800-285-3696
Broad choice of dependable bed linens, and every possible permutation of down comforters. Bedroom and bath accessories, towels, draperies, and window hardware. This reliable company will also custom-make shams, pillows, and bedcovers, or repair and refresh pillows and comforters.

CUDDLEDOWN OF MAINE
312 Canco Road
Portland, ME 04103
888-323-6793
De luxe European linens of the highest quality. Down comforters in four different warmth levels, pillows, towels, high-thread-count sheets

GARNET HILL
Box 262 Main Street
Franconia, NH 03580
800-622-6216
Originally, this catalogue offered only the coziest, thickest English cotton flannel sheets – and natural-fiber bed linens and sleepwear. They've branched out to bedroom draperies, dressers, classic fifties-style chairs, timeless bed styles, rugs, trundle beds, European bedroom slippers, bedside tables, blankets. Superb selection of towels and bathroom accessories.

HOLD EVERYTHING
P.O. Box 7807
San Francisco, CA 94120
800-421-2264
Extensive selections of storage, containers, and holders for everything from soap to towels, from shoes to laundry. Excellent range, fine quality.

HORCHOW
The Fine Linen Collection
P.O. Box 620048
Dallas, TX 75262
800-456-7000
Patterns with verve, colors that cheer. Best service: Supercale Plus cotton/poly percale in a choice of 20 colors – plus ginghams. Coordinated beds, plus bathroom basics.

MACY'S
P.O. Box 7888
San Francisco, CA 94120
800-622-9748
Excellent seasonal sales. Wide range of bedroom furniture, mattresses, pillows. Best-quality store-brand bed linens and towels.

THE NATURAL BEDROOM
P.O. Box 3071
Santa Rosa, CA 95402
800-365-6563
Natural-fiber, untreated, unbleached cottons, with Sonoma County wool stuffing, along with hand-tufted wool mattress toppers, and wool mattress pads. Elegantly simple maple bedroom furniture, plus natural linen sheets, paisley cotton damask untreated cotton sheets, pillowcases.

NEIMAN MARCUS BY MAIL
Fine Linens
P.O. Box 650589
Dallas, TX 75265
800-825-8000
Great luxuries, including Ralph Lauren's White Label Collection (590 thread-count Egyptian linens), cashmere throws, Ann Gish silk bed dressing, along with Italian linens. Great basics.

POTTERY BARN
P.O. Box 7044
San Francisco, CA 94120
Well-priced and well-made furniture and accessories. Seasonal selections of sheets, throws, rugs, vases, and now paint. Decorative draperies and window hardware.

SCHWEITZER LINEN
457 Columbus Avenue
New York, NY 10024
800-LLINENS (800-554-6367)
Family-run business offers finest-quality European linens. Subtle, tasteful designs.

CATALOGUE PHOTOGRAPHS
Special thanks to Waterworks for the photographs of the fine bathroom fittings, tiles, and fixtures featured in the California Catalogue section.

Michael Bruk
72, 77

Grey Crawford
12, 13, 28, 29, 35, 48, 54, 61,
80, 83, 86, 87, 95, 96, 97, 100,
102, 111

Mark Darley
14, 30, 39, 49, 52, 65, 94, 101

Scott Frances
69, 79, 82

Susan Gilmore
84

Thomas Heinser
47

Andrew Jacobson
60

John Jensen
78

David Livingston
18, 19, 32, 34, 36, 38, 43, 50, 57,
64, 66, 67, 88, 93, 105

Maura McEvoy
46, 99

Andrew McKinney
70L, 78

Colin McRae
8, 58, 116

Steven Mays
55

Jeremy Samuelson
1, 3, 68, 75, 90, 91, 92, 120

Brad Simmons
53

Tim Street-Porter
26, 81

Alex Vertikoff
74

Dominique Vorillon
10

David Wakely
98

Alan Weintraub
6, 16, 17, 20, 22, 23, 24, 25, 40, 56,
62, 63, 70R, 71, 73, 89, 103, 104

ACKNOWLEDGMENTS

It has been my great joy to work on this book.

San Francisco graphic designer Madeleine Corson has superb style, judgment, and focus.
She gave these pages their zing. Love and thanks.

I have had the great pleasure of working with outstanding photographers and interior designers, who
contributed their considerable talents to make this book both beautiful and inspirational.

I am especially grateful to California photographers Tim Street-Porter,
Alan Weintraub, Grey Crawford, Jeremy Samuelson, David Wakely, Mark Darley, Colin McRae,
David Livingston, Dominique Vorillon, and Michael Bruk.

Designers and architects with whom I have had the pleasure to work include Michael Berman,
Barbara Barry, Michael Smith, Jonathan Straley, Paul Wiseman, Eugene Nahemow and David Rivera, Michael Sant,
Dan Phipps, Douglas Durkin, Ann Jones, Suzanne Tucker, Gary Hutton, Mike Moore, Andrew Virtue, Stephen Brady,
Michael Tedrick, Cecilia Campa, Lou Ann Bauer, Orlando Diaz-Azcuy, Kate and Odom Stamps, Raun Thorp and Brian Tichenor,
Kerry Joyce, Joszi Meskan, Stephen Shubel, Kate McIntyre and Brad Huntzinger, and Myra Hoefer. Others who
have contributed their expertise include Lauren Berger, Ann Jones, Diana Brito, Joan and Steve Livingston,
Jill Pilaroscia, Melissa Deitz, and Theadora Van Runkle.

I look forward to working on many more books with my word-loving editor, Terry Ryan.

Bouquets to my special friends at Chronicle Books — Editor-in-Chief Nion McEvoy, Sarah McFall Bailey and
her extraordinary staff, Christina Wilson, Pamela Geismar, Dean Burrell, and Christine Carswell.

Heartfelt thanks.
Diane Dorrans Saeks

+≈+

AUTHOR

Diane Dorrans Saeks is a writer, editor, and lecturer who specializes in interior design, architecture, gardens,
travel, and fashion. She is the California editor for *Metropolitan Home,* a contributing editor for *Garden Design,*
San Francisco correspondent for *W* and *Women's Wear Daily,* and a frequent contributor to the *San Francisco Chronicle.*
Her articles have appeared in magazines and newspapers around the world, including *Vogue Living, Vogue Australia, In Style,*
the *New York Times,* the *Washington Post,* the *Los Angeles Times,* the *Times of London,* and the *Sydney Morning Herald.*
Her previous books include *California Wine Country, California Cottages, San Francisco Interiors, San Francisco: A Certain
Style, California Country, California Design Library: Living Rooms, California Design Library: Kitchens,* and
California Design Library: Bedrooms, all published by Chronicle Books. She lives in San Francisco.